FAITH &
BUSINESS

AN ENTREPRENEUR'S
WEEKLY DEVOTIONAL & JOURNAL

By David Mosberg

2025

Woodz Worx Publishing

Edited by M.G. Dowling
Illustrations and cover by Jeenalben Patel

First Printing: 2025

ISBN: 978-1-967464-42-5

Ordering Information:
Special discounts are available on quantity purchases by corporations, associations, educators, and others. For details, contact the publisher at the email listed below.

U.S. trade bookstores and wholesalers:

Please contact
david@triumvirfinancial.com

INTRODUCTION

Welcome to Faith & Business

A 52-Week Devotional for Christian Entrepreneurs and Business Leaders.

This devotional was born out of a simple but powerful truth:

YOUR BUSINESS IS YOUR MINISTRY!

Whether you're building a brand from scratch, managing a thriving company, freelancing, or leading a team, you are not just a business person — you are a Kingdom representative in the marketplace. You carry the light of Christ into boardrooms, coffee shops, contracts, spreadsheets, and customer service conversations. You are part of God's plan to transform culture, serve others, and create meaningful value—all through the work of your hands.

Yet this calling is not easy. Business can be lonely, risky, overwhelming, and often deeply personal. It's a world where faith is tested in practical ways: in late payments, employee tensions, quiet seasons, tough decisions, and the constant pressure to perform. That's why this devotional exists—to serve as a weekly anchor, helping you reconnect your business life with your spiritual life, so the two become one seamless expression of who you are in Christ.

God cares deeply about your work. Scripture is filled with builders, stewards, entrepreneurs, and marketplace leaders—from Abraham and Lydia to Nehemiah and the Proverbs 31 woman. These weren't just Sunday saints; they were everyday workers who honored God through faith-filled leadership, generosity, diligence, and trust. In the same way, you've been called to build, lead, serve, and create—on purpose and for a purpose.

Each of the 52 devotions in this guide is crafted to speak directly into the heart of that calling. Rooted in Scripture, each week will help you:

- Clarify your purpose
- Stay grounded in God's wisdom
- Navigate the tension between faith and ambition
- Cultivate rhythms of rest and trust
- Build a business culture that reflects Kingdom values
- Face real-life entrepreneurial challenges with boldness and grace

This devotional is not about adding another task to your to-do list. It's an invitation to partner with God in your business—not just occasionally, but intentionally and continually. It's a way to center your week on His Word, hear His voice in your decisions, and be reminded that success isn't measured by revenue alone—but by obedience, impact, and faithfulness.

So, whether you read these pages with your morning coffee, during your team meetings, or on your Sabbath day of rest, may they serve as a reminder: You are not alone. God is with you in every invoice, every decision, and every dream.

You are called. You are equipped. And through Christ, your business can be a powerful testimony to the world.

Welcome to the journey.

David Mosberg

DEVOTIONAL

HOW TO USE THIS DEVOTIONAL

Verse – A Scripture passage that grounds the week's focus.

Interpretation – A short explanation of the verse's meaning in the context of business.

Devotional Thought – A faith-filled reflection to stir your heart and mind for the week ahead.

Application – A challenge or practice to apply in your business.

Reflection – A reflection question for journaling or meditation.

Prayer – A prayer invites God into your leadership This is just an offering of words for those of us who need a place to start. Your prayer is YOUR prayer and conversation with God. Make it personal.

Each devotional is designed to guide you through a 5-part weekly rhythm:

SUGGESTED WEEKLY FLOW

- Read once at the beginning of your week (e.g., Monday morning).
- Reflect daily on the Scripture and question as situations arise.
- Journal midweek in the companion journal, using the reflection question and how it's playing out in real life.
- Pray intentionally through the closing prayer—make it your own.
- Revisit or share insights with a business partner, mentor, or group.

You can use this devotional privately or with a team. It also works well as a faith-based resource for Christian business groups or mastermind communities.

We have also created a companion journal to use each year so you can track your thoughts and evolution throughout your journey through business and spiritual maturity.

TABLE OF CONTENTS

This table of contents is designed to be used as a reference. Remember that a big part of bringing spirituality into your business is to build a relationship with God. In order to have a relationship, you may need to move around in the devotional to a topic that is relevant 'Right NOW!' not when you get to it in the sequence. Please use this table so you can easily find relevant topics, pray through them and bring them to the forefront of your focus so you can develop through them.

Introduction... III

How to Use This Devotional VI

Weekly Topics & Verses

Week 1 – Called to Create - Genesis 1:1..01

Week 2 – Trusting God's Timing - Ecclesiastes 3:1... 03

Week 3 – Stewardship, Not Ownership - Psalm 24:1....................................... 05

Week 4 – Planning with Purpose – Proverbs 16:3...07

Week 5 – Faith Over Fear – 2 Timothy 1:7... 09

Week 6 – Sabbath Rest for the Entrepreneur – Exodus 20:8 11

Week 7 – Serving Through Business – Mark 10:45.. 13

Week 8 – Integrity in Every Transaction – Proverbs 11:1.................................. 15

Week 9 – Leading with Wisdom – James 1:5...17

Week 10 – Financial Faithfulness – Luke 16:11... 19

Week 11 – Overcoming Burnout – Matthew 11:28... 21

Week 12 – Clarity in Vision – Habakkuk 2:2 23

Week 13 – God's Favor in Hard Seasons – Genesis 39:2 25

Week 14 – The Power of Small Things – Zechariah 4:10...................................27

Week 15 – Speaking Life Over Your Business – Proverbs 18:21.......................29

Week 16 – Generosity as a Strategy – 2 Corinthians 9:6................................. 31

Week 17 – Excellence, Not Perfection – Colossians 3:23..................................33

TABLE OF CONTENTS continued

Week 18 – Making Room for Margin – Mark 6:31...35

Week 19 – God Is Your Source – Philippians 4:19...37

Week 20 – Courage to Take the Next Step – Joshua 1:9.................................39

Week 21 – The Company You Keep – Proverbs 13:20.......................................41

Week 22 – Humility in Leadership – Philippians 2:3...43

Week 23 – Dealing with Disappointment – Psalm 34:18..................................45

Week 24 – Faithfulness Over Flash – Matthew 25:23.......................................47

Week 25 – Waiting with Purpose – Isaiah 40:31..49

Week 26 – Creating a Culture of Honor – Romans 12:10..................................51

Week 27 – Trusting God with the Outcome – Proverbs 3:5-6..........................53

Week 28 – Integrity in the Details – Luke 16:10..55

Week 29 – When You Feel Stuck – Psalm 37:23-24...57

Week 30 – Kingdom-Minded Metrics – Matthew 6:33......................................59

Week 31 – The Power of Encouragement – Hebrews 10:24..............................61

Week 32 – Rejoice in Suffering – Romans – 5:3-4...63

Week 33 – When You Feel Overlooked – Galatians 6:9.....................................65

Week 34 – The Blessing of Boundaries – Proverbs 4:23 67

Week 35 – God's Timing Is Perfect – Ecclesiastes 3:11....................................69

Week 36 – Stewarding Your Gifts – 1 Peter 4:10...71

Week 37 – Establish the Work of Our Hands – Psalm 90:17.............................73

Week 38 – Strength for the Journey – Philippians 4:13 75

Week 39 – God Sees Your Integrity– Proverbs 28:6 77

Week 40 – Planted and Prosperous – Psalm 1:3 79

Week 41 – Building Legacy, Not Just Income – Proverbs 13:22.......................81

Week 42 – The Cost of Compromise – Proverbs 10:9..83

TABLE OF CONTENTS continued

Week 43 – Delegating with Trust – Exodus 18:21...85

Week 44 – Staying Grateful in Growth – 1 Thessalonians 5:18.......................... 87

Week 45 – Renew your Mind – Romans 12:2 89

Week 46 – Profit with Purpose – Deuteronomy 8:18.. 91

Week 47 – Rejection Is Not the End – Isaiah 41:10 93

Week 48 – Vision for the Future – Proverbs 29:18..95

Week 49 – A Heart for Generosity – 2 Corinthians 9:7.. 97

Week 50 – Restoring What's Been Lost – Joel 2:25 99

Week 51 – The Power of Your Testimony – Revelation 12:11 101

Week 52 – Finish Faithfully, Start Fresh – Philippians 1:6.................................103

A Personal Note of Thanks from the Author...105

VERSE

GENESIS 1:1 – *"In the beginning God created..."*

INTERPRETATION

The very first verse of the Bible reveals a fundamental truth about God—He is a Creator. This foundational act sets the tone for all of Scripture and life itself. As His image-bearers (Genesis 1:27), we are endowed with the capacity and calling to be creators as well. Creativity isn't limited to the arts—it's reflected in innovation, problem-solving, building systems, and launching businesses.

DEVOTIONAL THOUGHT

God is the original Creator, and as image-bearers, we too are called to create. Your business is not just a livelihood—it's an expression of God's creativity through you. Begin this process by dedicating your work to Him.

APPLICATION

As entrepreneurs, we have a unique opportunity to mirror God's creativity in the marketplace. Whether you're developing a new product, designing a customer experience, or cultivating a team culture, you are reflecting the Creator's nature. Let your business be a light, a testimony to the order, beauty, and purpose God displays in creation. When faced with obstacles or the need for innovation, seek God's wisdom—He delights in guiding His co-creators.

REFLECTION

How is your business a reflection of God's creative nature? Are you limiting your mind on what you are able to create? Breakthrough the human boundaries and bring God into your ideas and let them expand past your limitations!

PRAYER

Heavenly Father, Thank You for being the original Creator and for forming me in Your image. Thank You for entrusting me with the opportunity to create through my business. Help me to honor You in how I build, serve, and innovate. May I walk in step with Your Spirit and dedicate every part of this venture to You. Inspire me to reflect Your beauty and order in all that I do. In Jesus' Name, Amen.

WEEK 1

SCRIPTURE FOCUS
GENESIS 1:1 – "In the beginning God created..."
What part of this week's verse stood out to you the most?

_____

_____

_____

MAIN INSIGHT OR TAKEAWAY
What truth or lesson did God highlight for you through the devotional?

_____

_____

_____

PERSONAL APPLICATION
How will you apply this to your business or leadership this week?

_____

_____

_____

CHALLENGES OR CONVICTIONS
Did anything convict, challenge, or stretch you?

_____

_____

_____

ANSWERED PRAYERS / PRAISE REPORT
Did you see God show up in any way this week?

_____

_____

_____

PRAYER FOR THE WEEK
Write a personal prayer based on your reflection.

_____

_____

_____

NEXT STEP OR ACTION ITEM
What's one specific action you'll take based on this reflection?

_____

_____

_____

VERSE

ECCLESIASTES 3:1 – *"There is a time for everything, and a season for every activity under the heavens."*

INTERPRETATION

Life and business are filled with seasons—some of growth, some of waiting. God's timing is not always our timing, but it is always perfect. Recognizing His sovereignty allows us to rest in the in–between moments and trust that He is working all things together for our good.

DEVOTIONAL THOUGHT

Entrepreneurship often brings seasons of uncertainty. Whether waiting on funding, clients, or clarity, God calls us to trust His timeline over our own. This may be one of the hardest disciplines to conquer, particularly as an ambitious natured person. Pay attention to how God communicates with you and you WILL be able to fall in to his perfect plan!

APPLICATION

Instead of pushing ahead in your own strength, take time this week to pray over areas where you feel delayed or stalled. Ask God to reveal His purpose in the waiting and align your expectations with His will. Your delay may be His divine setup. Prepare yourself to be Blessed by the answers God provides.

REFLECTION

Are you anxious about something in your business that needs surrendering to God's timing? Time to Pray!

PRAYER

Lord,I trust in Your perfect timing. I confess my impatience and desire for immediate results. Remind me that You see the full picture and that Your timing will always be best for me and my business. I rest in your peace knowing You are never late. Amen.

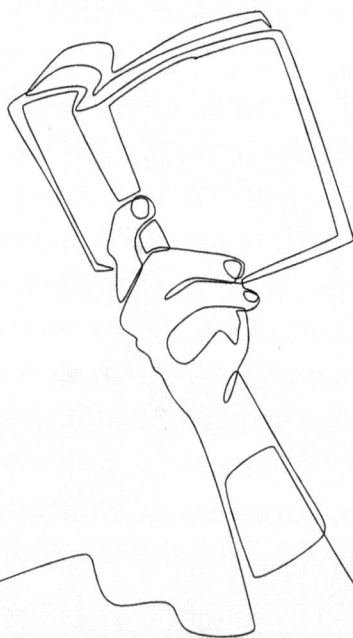

SCRIPTURE FOCUS

ECCLESIASTES 3:1 – "There is a time for everything, and a season for every activity under the heavens."
What part of this week's verse stood out to you the most?

MAIN INSIGHT OR TAKEAWAY

What truth or lesson did God highlight for you through the devotional?

PERSONAL APPLICATION

How will you apply this to your business or leadership this week?

CHALLENGES OR CONVICTIONS

Did anything convict, challenge, or stretch you?

ANSWERED PRAYERS / PRAISE REPORT

Did you see God show up in any way this week?

PRAYER FOR THE WEEK

Write a personal prayer based on your reflection.

NEXT STEP OR ACTION ITEM

What's one specific action you'll take based on this reflection?

WEEK 3 | STEWARDSHIP, NOT OWNERSHIP

VERSE

PSALM 24:1 – *"The earth is the Lord's, and everything in it, the world, and all who live in it."*

INTERPRETATION

Everything we have—our time, talent, and treasure—belongs to God. We are not owners but stewards, entrusted with His resources to manage them faithfully.

DEVOTIONAL THOUGHT

Your business, your team, your finances—all belong to God. Viewing yourself as a steward rather than an owner changes how you lead, plan, and serve. Don't procrastinate on God's work or in his business.

APPLICATION

Evaluate your business decisions this week. Are you managing God's resources with integrity and care? What would change if you acted more like a steward and less like the ultimate authority?

REFLECTION

How can you better steward the finances, time, and relationships in your business? Are you holding back on something that God wants you to move forward on because you are forgetting that he's got you? Remember that all things are possible in HIS business.

PRAYER

Father,
I acknowledge that everything I have is Yours. Teach me to be a wise steward of the business You've entrusted to me. I purpose to manage it with excellence, humility, and a heart that seeks Your glory, not my own. In Jesus' Name.
Amen.

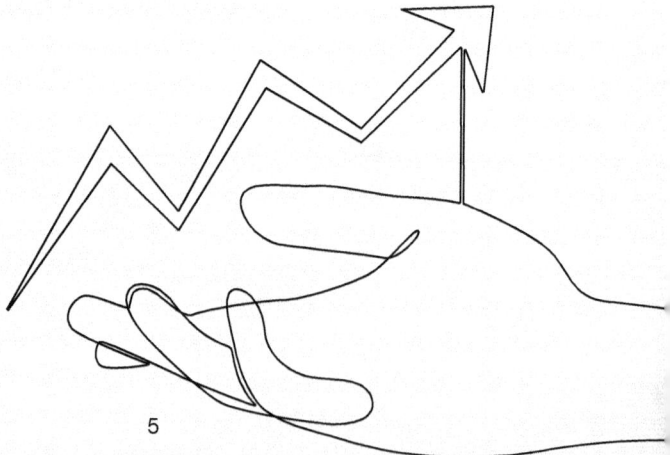

SCRIPTURE FOCUS

PSALM 24:1 – "The earth is the Lord's, and everything in it, the world, and all who live in it."
What part of this week's verse stood out to you the most?

_____

_____

_____

MAIN INSIGHT OR TAKEAWAY

What truth or lesson did God highlight for you through the devotional?

_____

_____

_____

PERSONAL APPLICATION

How will you apply this to your business or leadership this week?

_____

_____

_____

CHALLENGES OR CONVICTIONS

Did anything convict, challenge, or stretch you?

_____

_____

_____

ANSWERED PRAYERS / PRAISE REPORT

Did you see God show up in any way this week?

_____

_____

_____

PRAYER FOR THE WEEK

Write a personal prayer based on your reflection.

_____

_____

_____

NEXT STEP OR ACTION ITEM

What's one specific action you'll take based on this reflection?

_____

_____

_____

VERSE:

PROVERBS 16:3 – *"Commit to the Lord whatever you do, and he will establish your plans."*

INTERPRETATION

When we bring our plans before the Lord and submit them to His will, He aligns our vision with His. Our success is not determined by effort alone, but by our willingness to commit everything to God.

DEVOTIONAL THOUGHT

God honors our diligence, but He desires our dependence even more. Your planning process should start with prayer, not just end with it.

APPLICATION

Before drafting your next business strategy or launching a new initiative, take time to seek God. Pray over your calendar, goals, and vision. Let Him direct your steps and provide wisdom.

REFLECTION

How do you sense God directing you and your business? How is your business fulfilling God's plans for your life? Are you being intentional with your time and resources?

PRAYER

Lord,

I submit my plans, goals, and dreams to You. Lead me in the way I should go, and help me trust Your guidance over my own understanding. Let everything, I plan be filtered through the lens of Your purpose.

Amen.

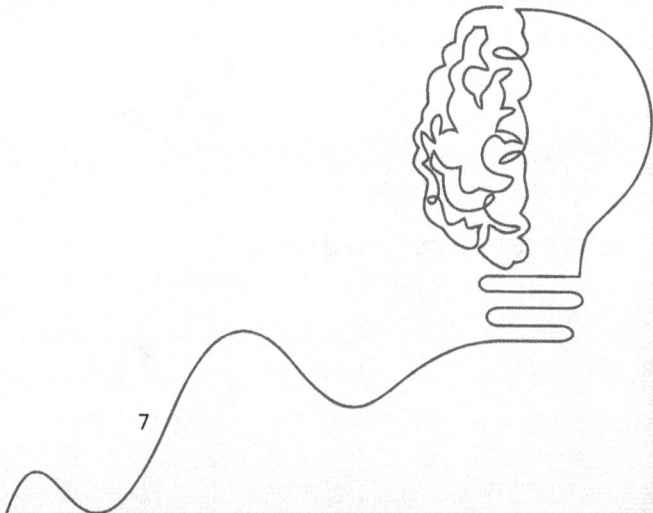

WEEK 4

SCRIPTURE FOCUS
PROVERBS 16:3 – "Commit to the Lord whatever you do, and he will establish your plans."
What part of this week's verse stood out to you the most?

MAIN INSIGHT OR TAKEAWAY
What truth or lesson did God highlight for you through the devotional?

PERSONAL APPLICATION
How will you apply this to your business or leadership this week?

CHALLENGES OR CONVICTIONS
Did anything convict, challenge, or stretch you?

ANSWERED PRAYERS / PRAISE REPORT
Did you see God show up in any way this week?

PRAYER FOR THE WEEK
Write a personal prayer based on your reflection.

NEXT STEP OR ACTION ITEM
What's one specific action you'll take based on this reflection?

VERSE

TIMOTHY 1:7 (KJV) – *"For God has not given us a spirit of fear, but of power and of love and of a sound mind."*

INTERPRETATION

Fear is not from God. It's a spiritual distraction that clouds our decision-making, stifles innovation, and causes us to act from scarcity instead of trust. God replaces fear with His own nature—power, love, and a sound, disciplined mind—so we can lead boldly and faithfully.

DEVOTIONAL THOUGHT

Fear shows up in entrepreneurship often—fear of failure, fear of rejection, fear of the unknown. Some of us also suffer from the 'Imposter Syndrome'. But God doesn't expect us to white-knuckle our way through business. He equips us with everything we need to walk in courage and clarity. The more we focus on His power and promises, the less control fear has over our lives.

APPLICATION

Identify one area where fear may be influencing your decisions. Are you avoiding growth, delaying action, or hesitating to speak truth because of fear? This week, choose one fear and bring it to God in prayer. Then take one small, obedient step forward in faith.

REFLECTION

What fear do you need to surrender so you can walk in God's power, love, and wisdom this week? Remember who your Father is and the family you are a part of. You are even more than you can imagine in his image!

PRAYER

Lord,
I confess that fear often creeps into my thinking and clouds my leadership. Help me recognize fear for what it is—not from You. Thank you for filling me with Your power, love, and clarity. Continue to strengthen me to move forward in faith especially when the path feels uncertain. In Jesus' Name, Amen.

SCRIPTURE FOCUS

TIMOTHY 1:7 (KJV) – "For God has not given us a spirit of fear, but of power and of love and of a sound mind."
What part of this week's verse stood out to you the most?

MAIN INSIGHT OR TAKEAWAY

What truth or lesson did God highlight for you through the devotional?

PERSONAL APPLICATION

How will you apply this to your business or leadership this week?

CHALLENGES OR CONVICTIONS

Did anything convict, challenge, or stretch you?

ANSWERED PRAYERS / PRAISE REPORT

Did you see God show up in any way this week?

PRAYER FOR THE WEEK

Write a personal prayer based on your reflection.

NEXT STEP OR ACTION ITEM

What's one specific action you'll take based on this reflection?

VERSE

EXODUS 20:8 – *"Remember the Sabbath day by keeping it holy."*

INTERPRETATION

The Sabbath is not just a day off—it's a divine rhythm instituted by God. It's a reminder that our value doesn't come from constant productivity. Observing the Sabbath is a weekly declaration of trust in God's provision and a discipline that aligns us with His pace and priorities.

DEVOTIONAL THOUGHT

Entrepreneurs often wear busyness as a badge of honor. But God calls us to rest, not just for recovery but for worship, renewal, and realignment. The Sabbath reorients our hearts toward what matters most. It teaches us to rely on God's sufficiency rather than our striving.

APPLICATION

This week, schedule intentional time for Sabbath. Not just a day without work—but a day set apart to rest in God's presence, enjoy your relationships, and reflect on His goodness. Let the act of resting be an expression of trust that He's still in control, even when you're not producing.

REFLECTION

Are you honoring the Sabbath in a way that brings spiritual, emotional, and physical renewal?

PRAYER

Father,
Forgive me for the times I've ignored Your invitation to rest. I confess that I often equate busyness with value. I commit to reclaiming the Sabbath as holy—set apart to be with You. Teach me to slow down, breathe deeply, and remember that You are the source of all provision and peace.
Amen.

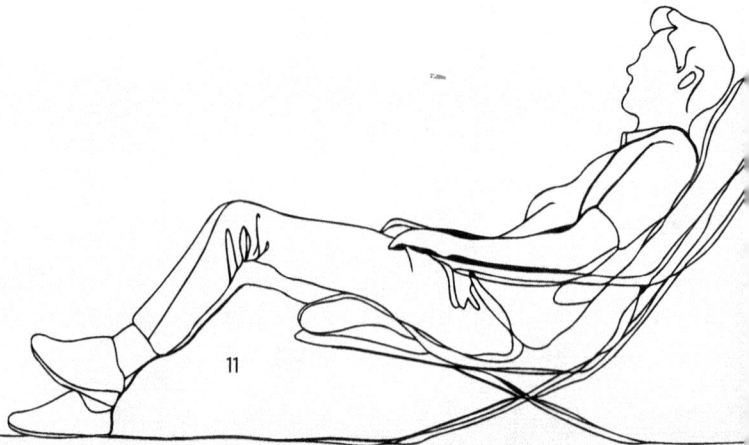

WEEK 6

SCRIPTURE FOCUS
EXODUS 20:8 – "Remember the Sabbath day by keeping it holy."
What part of this week's verse stood out to you the most?

_____

_____

_____

MAIN INSIGHT OR TAKEAWAY
What truth or lesson did God highlight for you through the devotional?

_____

_____

_____

PERSONAL APPLICATION
How will you apply this to your business or leadership this week?

_____

_____

_____

CHALLENGES OR CONVICTIONS
Did anything convict, challenge, or stretch you?

_____

_____

_____

ANSWERED PRAYERS / PRAISE REPORT
Did you see God show up in any way this week?

_____

_____

_____

PRAYER FOR THE WEEK
Write a personal prayer based on your reflection.

_____

_____

_____

NEXT STEP OR ACTION ITEM
What's one specific action you'll take based on this reflection?

_____

_____

_____

VERSE

MARK 10:45 — *"For even the Son of Man did not come to be served, but to serve, and to give his life as a ransom for many."*

INTERPRETATION

Jesus, though fully God, humbled Himself to serve others. His leadership style was radical—not about power or position, but about meeting needs and elevating others. True greatness in the Kingdom comes through service.

DEVOTIONAL THOUGHT

In business, it's tempting to lead for personal gain—profit, prestige, or control. But when you view your business as a ministry, service becomes your driving force. Whether you're helping clients, mentoring staff, or supporting your community, you reflect Christ when you serve with humility and excellence.

APPLICATION

Look for a new way to serve this week and in the weeks to come—beyond what's expected. Surprise a client with generosity, write a note of encouragement to a team member, or offer time or resources to someone in need. Let your business be known for how it serves, not just how it sells.

REFLECTION

Who can you serve through your business this week, and how?

PRAYER

Jesus,

You modeled servant leadership so powerfully. Teach me to lead with that same spirit. Let my business reflect Your heart—to serve, to bless, and to lift others up. I commit to building a culture of service in every part of my work.

Amen.

SCRIPTURE FOCUS

MARK 10:45 – "For even the Son of Man did not come to be served, but to serve, and to give his life as a ransom for many."

What part of this week's verse stood out to you the most?

_____

_____

MAIN INSIGHT OR TAKEAWAY

What truth or lesson did God highlight for you through the devotional?

_____

_____

_____

PERSONAL APPLICATION

How will you apply this to your business or leadership this week?

_____

_____

_____

CHALLENGES OR CONVICTIONS

Did anything convict, challenge, or stretch you?

_____

_____

_____

ANSWERED PRAYERS / PRAISE REPORT

Did you see God show up in any way this week?

_____

_____

_____

PRAYER FOR THE WEEK

Write a personal prayer based on your reflection.

_____

_____

_____

NEXT STEP OR ACTION ITEM

What's one specific action you'll take based on this reflection?

_____

_____

_____

VERSE:

PROVERBS 11:1 – *"The Lord detests dishonest scales, but accurate weights find favor with him."*

INTERPRETATION

In ancient marketplaces, scales were easily rigged to cheat buyers. God despises dishonesty in business. But He delights in integrity—fairness, transparency, and truth—because it reflects His character.

DEVOTIONAL THOUGHT

Integrity isn't just about major decisions—it's about everyday practices. From contracts to pricing, hiring to marketing, God calls us to a higher standard. When we operate with integrity, we earn trust, build strong reputations, and honor God in ways that endure beyond our success.

APPLICATION

Do a quick audit this week. Are there any practices in your business that need adjustment to align with God's standard of honesty? Speak truth even when it costs you. Choose fairness even when it feels like you're falling behind. God will bless the path of integrity.

REFLECTION

Is there an area in your business where God is calling you to higher integrity? Make sure you surround yourself with Godly ambassadors to help hold you to the standards of integrity that God would expect in his business.

PRAYER

Lord,

Let truth and integrity be the foundation of my business. I commit to resisting shortcuts and compromise. Teach me to do what's right, even when no one is watching. My work reflects Your righteousness and draws others to trust in You.

Amen.

SCRIPTURE FOCUS
PROVERBS 11:1 – "The Lord detests dishonest scales, but accurate weights find favor with him."
What part of this week's verse stood out to you the most?

_____
_____
_____

MAIN INSIGHT OR TAKEAWAY
What truth or lesson did God highlight for you through the devotional?

_____
_____
_____

PERSONAL APPLICATION
How will you apply this to your business or leadership this week?

_____
_____
_____

CHALLENGES OR CONVICTIONS
Did anything convict, challenge, or stretch you?

_____
_____
_____

ANSWERED PRAYERS / PRAISE REPORT
Did you see God show up in any way this week?

_____
_____
_____

PRAYER FOR THE WEEK
Write a personal prayer based on your reflection.

_____
_____
_____

NEXT STEP OR ACTION ITEM
What's one specific action you'll take based on this reflection?

_____
_____
_____

VERSE

JAMES 1:5 – *"If any of you lacks wisdom, you should ask God, who gives generously to all without finding fault, and it will be given to you."*

INTERPRETATION

God doesn't shame us for lacking wisdom—He invites us to seek it. Divine wisdom is practical, spiritual, and often countercultural. It equips us to make decisions rooted in truth, not just trends.

DEVOTIONAL THOUGHT

Leadership in business brings daily challenges—conflicts to resolve, choices to make, people to guide. God promises to generously supply wisdom when we ask. His insight isn't just for Sunday sermons—it's for strategic plans, client conversations, and contract decisions.

APPLICATION

What's a current situation where you feel uncertain? Pause and invite God into it. Ask for His wisdom—not just information, but discernment. Then act in faith, knowing He's guiding you even when the way isn't fully clear.

REFLECTION

What specific area of your business leadership needs God's wisdom today?

PRAYER

Father,
I acknowledge that I don't always know the right path, but You do. I ask for Your wisdom to lead with grace, confidence, and clarity. I listen for Your voice to follow You above the noise of my own ambition or fear.
Amen.

SCRIPTURE FOCUS

JAMES 1:5 – "If any of you lacks wisdom, you should ask God, who gives generously to all without finding fault, and it will be given to you."

What part of this week's verse stood out to you the most?

_____

_____

MAIN INSIGHT OR TAKEAWAY

What truth or lesson did God highlight for you through the devotional?

_____

_____

_____

PERSONAL APPLICATION

How will you apply this to your business or leadership this week?

_____

_____

_____

CHALLENGES OR CONVICTIONS

Did anything convict, challenge, or stretch you?

_____

_____

_____

ANSWERED PRAYERS / PRAISE REPORT

Did you see God show up in any way this week?

_____

_____

_____

PRAYER FOR THE WEEK

Write a personal prayer based on your reflection.

_____

_____

_____

NEXT STEP OR ACTION ITEM

What's one specific action you'll take based on this reflection?

_____

_____

_____

VERSE

LUKE 16:11 – *"So if you have not been trustworthy in handling worldly wealth, who will trust you with true riches?"*

INTERPRETATION

How we handle money reveals our spiritual maturity. Faithfulness with finances—no matter the amount—is a prerequisite for greater responsibilities in God's Kingdom.

DEVOTIONAL THOUGHT

Business finances are not separate from your walk with God. How you budget, price, save, give, and invest matters to Him. Faithfulness doesn't mean having more; it means being intentional with what you already have.

APPLICATION

Take time this week to review your financial stewardship. Are you tracking wisely? Giving generously? Making decisions that reflect trust in God rather than fear or greed? Ask Him to help you steward well.

REFLECTION

Is there a financial area of your business where God is calling you to greater faithfulness? This is a great opportunity to also peek into your home and how you are doing as a leader in your home with your finances as well.

PRAYER

Lord,
Thank You for the resources You've entrusted to me. I commit to honoring You in how I manage money—in big decisions and small ones. Teach me to live open-handed and faithfully, knowing it all belongs to You.
Amen.

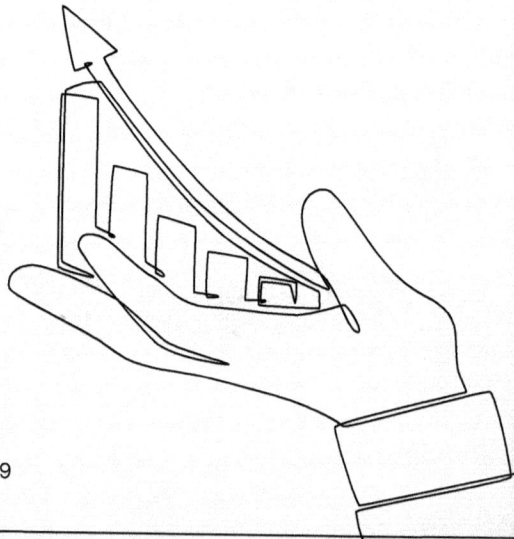

WEEK 10

SCRIPTURE FOCUS
LUKE 16:11 – "So if you have not been trustworthy in handling worldly wealth, who will trust you with true riches?"
What part of this week's verse stood out to you the most?

_____

_____

_____

MAIN INSIGHT OR TAKEAWAY
What truth or lesson did God highlight for you through the devotional?

_____

_____

_____

PERSONAL APPLICATION
How will you apply this to your business or leadership this week?

_____

_____

_____

CHALLENGES OR CONVICTIONS
Did anything convict, challenge, or stretch you?

_____

_____

_____

ANSWERED PRAYERS / PRAISE REPORT
Did you see God show up in any way this week?

_____

_____

_____

PRAYER FOR THE WEEK
Write a personal prayer based on your reflection.

_____

_____

_____

NEXT STEP OR ACTION ITEM
What's one specific action you'll take based on this reflection?

_____

_____

_____

VERSE:

MATTHEW 11:28 – *"Come to me, all you who are weary and burdened, and I will give you rest."*

INTERPRETATION

Jesus doesn't just offer eternal life—He offers daily rest for our weary souls. His invitation is personal and healing. He doesn't require hustle; He calls us to abide.

DEVOTIONAL THOUGHT

Entrepreneurs often feel pressure to do it all. But burnout isn't a badge of honor—it's a sign we're operating outside of God's design. Rest is not weakness. It's wisdom. When we come to Jesus regularly, we find renewed strength and clarity.

APPLICATION

What has you worn out this week? Write it down. Then ask Jesus to carry it with you. Build in daily pauses—even five minutes of silence or prayer—and practice regular rhythms of retreat to reconnect with Him. Remember, this feeling may be coming for the need for a season of change.

REFLECTION

What burdens from the past or present are you carrying alone that Jesus is inviting you to surrender? Perhaps it's an old wound, an unspoken fear, or the weight of expectations you can't seem to meet. Jesus does not ask you to pretend it isn't there—He invites you to place it in His care.

PRAYER

Jesus,
I bring You my tired body and overwhelmed heart. I rest in You—not just on weekends, but in each moment. You restore my soul so I can work from a place of peace, not pressure.
Amen.

WEEK 11

SCRIPTURE FOCUS
MATTHEW 11:28 – "Come to me, all you who are weary and burdened, and I will give you rest."
What part of this week's verse stood out to you the most?

_____
_____
_____

MAIN INSIGHT OR TAKEAWAY
What truth or lesson did God highlight for you through the devotional?

_____
_____
_____

PERSONAL APPLICATION
How will you apply this to your business or leadership this week?

_____
_____
_____

CHALLENGES OR CONVICTIONS
Did anything convict, challenge, or stretch you?

_____
_____
_____

ANSWERED PRAYERS / PRAISE REPORT
Did you see God show up in any way this week?

_____
_____
_____

PRAYER FOR THE WEEK
Write a personal prayer based on your reflection.

_____
_____
_____

NEXT STEP OR ACTION ITEM
What's one specific action you'll take based on this reflection?

_____
_____
_____

VERSE

HABAKKUK 2:2 – (ESV) *"Write the vision; make it plain on tablets, so he may run who reads it"*

INTERPRETATION

God values clarity. A clear vision isn't just for you—it's for those who follow you, work with you, and are impacted by your business. Vision fuels purpose, and purpose fuels endurance.

DEVOTIONAL THOUGHT

Without vision, your business drifts. With vision, you run. As a leader, it's your responsibility to define and communicate the "why" behind the work. A God-given vision inspires excellence and keeps you grounded when challenges come.

APPLICATION

Revisit your business vision this week. Is it clear, Christ-centered, and compelling? Can your team articulate it? Is it written down and prayed over regularly? If not, it's time to refocus.

REFLECTION

What part of your business vision needs refinement—or bold re-commitment? Do you have a plan to go with your vision?

PRAYER

God,
You are the source of vision and direction. Help me write the vision You've placed in my heart, and lead me to pursue it with faith and focus. Make it clear, make it fruitful, and help me steward it well. Amen.

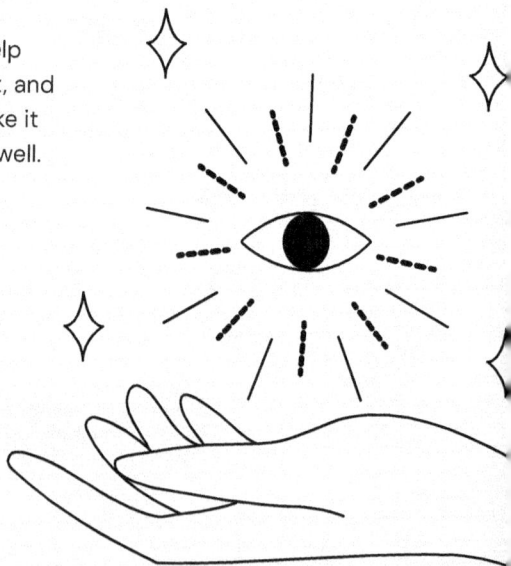

WEEK 12

SCRIPTURE FOCUS

HABAKKUK 2:2 – (ESV) "Write the vision; make it plain on tablets, so he may run who reads it"

What part of this week's verse stood out to you the most?

MAIN INSIGHT OR TAKEAWAY

What truth or lesson did God highlight for you through the devotional?

PERSONAL APPLICATION

How will you apply this to your business or leadership this week?

CHALLENGES OR CONVICTIONS

Did anything convict, challenge, or stretch you?

ANSWERED PRAYERS / PRAISE REPORT

Did you see God show up in any way this week?

PRAYER FOR THE WEEK

Write a personal prayer based on your reflection.

NEXT STEP OR ACTION ITEM

What's one specific action you'll take based on this reflection?

VERSE

GENESIS 39:2 – *"The Lord was with Joseph so that he prospered, and he lived in the house of his Egyptian master."*

INTERPRETATION

Joseph's success wasn't because of ideal circumstances—it was because of God's presence. Even in slavery and prison, the Lord's favor was upon him. Favor isn't about comfort—it's about God's hand on your work.

DEVOTIONAL THOUGHT

Business doesn't always go as planned. Sometimes, despite our best efforts, things break down or fall short. But God doesn't leave us in hard seasons—He works through them with us. His favor may not remove the challenge, but it will sustain you through it.

APPLICATION

This week, if you're facing setbacks or discouragement, pause and ask: "Where is God still at work?" Look for His favor in unexpected places—through relationships, lessons, or provision that sustain you. Stay faithful where you are, and trust that He's building something beyond your sight.

REFLECTION

What current hardship can you reframe as a place where God is still with you? Where will you look to find him?

PRAYER

Lord,
Even in the hard places, You are with me. I trust in Your presence more than in my performance. Let me see Your favor not just in outcomes, but in how You walk with me through every season. Amen.

WEEK 13

SCRIPTURE FOCUS

GENESIS 39:2 – "The Lord was with Joseph so that he prospered, and he lived in the house of his Egyptian master."
What part of this week's verse stood out to you the most?

_____
_____
_____

MAIN INSIGHT OR TAKEAWAY

What truth or lesson did God highlight for you through the devotional?

_____
_____
_____

PERSONAL APPLICATION

How will you apply this to your business or leadership this week?

_____
_____
_____

CHALLENGES OR CONVICTIONS

Did anything convict, challenge, or stretch you?

_____
_____
_____

ANSWERED PRAYERS / PRAISE REPORT

Did you see God show up in any way this week?

_____
_____
_____

PRAYER FOR THE WEEK

Write a personal prayer based on your reflection.

_____
_____
_____

NEXT STEP OR ACTION ITEM

What's one specific action you'll take based on this reflection?

_____
_____
_____

VERSE

ZECHARIAH 4:10 (NLT) – *"Do not despise these small beginnings, for the Lord rejoices to see the work begin."*

INTERPRETATION

God celebrates the start of a vision, even when it's small and unimpressive to the world. Every great work begins with a humble step of obedience.

DEVOTIONAL THOUGHT

In business, it's easy to compare your progress to others. You may feel like your reach is small, your revenue is light, or your vision is slow to grow. But God rejoices in your faithfulness. The work you do in private—serving one client well, refining a system, honoring your word—matters deeply.

APPLICATION

This week, shift your focus from "how big is it?" to "how faithful am I?" Embrace the process of building slowly and well. Be encouraged that God sees your small beginnings and rejoices in your obedience.

REFLECTION

What "small" thing in your business can you celebrate and be faithful with this week? If you have a team, this would be a great exercise to share.

PRAYER

God,
Thank You for rejoicing over my beginnings. I commit
to not measure my business by worldly standards,
but by Your pleasure. Together we build with patience,
persistence, and joy—even when it feels small.
Amen.

SCRIPTURE FOCUS

ZECHARIAH 4:10 (NLT) – "Do not despise these small beginnings, for the Lord rejoices to see the work begin."

What part of this week's verse stood out to you the most?

_____
_____
_____

MAIN INSIGHT OR TAKEAWAY

What truth or lesson did God highlight for you through the devotional?

_____
_____
_____

PERSONAL APPLICATION

How will you apply this to your business or leadership this week?

_____
_____
_____

CHALLENGES OR CONVICTIONS

Did anything convict, challenge, or stretch you?

_____
_____
_____

ANSWERED PRAYERS / PRAISE REPORT

Did you see God show up in any way this week?

_____
_____
_____

PRAYER FOR THE WEEK

Write a personal prayer based on your reflection.

_____
_____
_____

NEXT STEP OR ACTION ITEM

What's one specific action you'll take based on this reflection?

_____
_____
_____

VERSE

PROVERBS 18:21 – *"The tongue has the power of life and death, and those who love it will eat its fruit."*

INTERPRETATION

Words shape reality. They influence the atmosphere of your business, the morale of your team, and your own mindset. God has given us the ability to speak life—or discouragement—into the environments we lead.

DEVOTIONAL THOUGHT

As a business owner or leader, your words matter. What you declare over your team, your goals, and yourself becomes a powerful force. When we align our words with faith instead of fear, we invite God's perspective into our daily work.

APPLICATION

Be intentional this week about what you say out loud and to yourself! Bless your business with prayer. Speak encouragement over your team. Replace negative or anxious thoughts with words rooted in Scripture and truth. Watch how the spiritual climate shifts.

REFLECTION

What words have you been speaking about your business—and are they words of life? Pick one thing each day this week to speak LIFE into your business.

PRAYER

Lord,

I choose to be a leader who speaks life. Let my words reflect faith, not fear; truth, not anxiety. Teach me to declare Your promises over my business and speak encouragement over those I lead.

Amen.

SCRIPTURE FOCUS

PROVERBS 18:21 – "The tongue has the power of life and death, and those who love it will eat its fruit."
What part of this week's verse stood out to you the most?

MAIN INSIGHT OR TAKEAWAY

What truth or lesson did God highlight for you through the devotional?

PERSONAL APPLICATION

How will you apply this to your business or leadership this week?

CHALLENGES OR CONVICTIONS

Did anything convict, challenge, or stretch you?

ANSWERED PRAYERS / PRAISE REPORT

Did you see God show up in any way this week?

PRAYER FOR THE WEEK

Write a personal prayer based on your reflection.

NEXT STEP OR ACTION ITEM

What's one specific action you'll take based on this reflection?

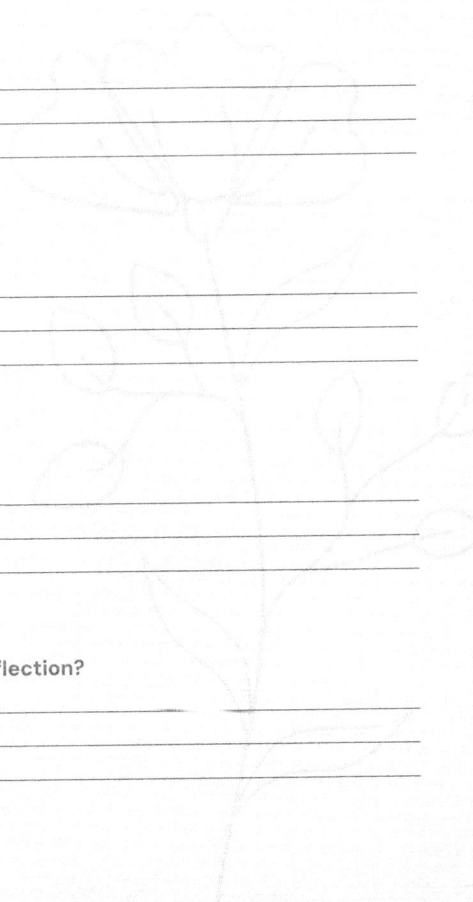

VERSE

2 CORINTHIANS 9:6 — *"Whoever sows sparingly will also reap sparingly, and whoever sows generously will also reap generously."*

INTERPRETATION

In God's Kingdom, generosity isn't a loss—it's an investment. God honors a generous heart, and He multiplies what we give when it's sown in faith.

DEVOTIONAL THOUGHT

It's tempting to hold tightly to resources, especially in lean seasons. But generosity in business—whether through giving, mentoring, time, or care—positions you to partner with how God works. It builds trust, attracts loyalty, and opens doors you didn't earn.

APPLICATION

Identify one area this week where you can sow generously. It might be giving financially, offering your services, investing in a staff member, or supporting another entrepreneur. Don't wait to give until you "have more"—start now with what's in your hand.

REFLECTION

Where is God prompting you to sow generously—even if it feels small?

PRAYER

God,

You are the Giver of all good things. I commit to be generous like You. Help me loosen my grip and trust that what I sow in faith, You will multiply for Your glory and others' good. Amen.

WEEK 16

SCRIPTURE FOCUS

2 CORINTHIANS 9:6 – "Whoever sows sparingly will also reap sparingly, and whoever sows generously will also reap generously."

What part of this week's verse stood out to you the most?

_____

_____

MAIN INSIGHT OR TAKEAWAY

What truth or lesson did God highlight for you through the devotional?

_____

_____

_____

PERSONAL APPLICATION

How will you apply this to your business or leadership this week?

_____

_____

_____

CHALLENGES OR CONVICTIONS

Did anything convict, challenge, or stretch you?

_____

_____

_____

ANSWERED PRAYERS / PRAISE REPORT

Did you see God show up in any way this week?

_____

_____

_____

PRAYER FOR THE WEEK

Write a personal prayer based on your reflection.

_____

_____

_____

NEXT STEP OR ACTION ITEM

What's one specific action you'll take based on this reflection?

_____

_____

_____

VERSE

COLOSSIANS 3:23 – *"Whatever you do, work at it with all your heart, as working for the Lord, not for human masters."*

INTERPRETATION

God calls us to wholehearted work—not to impress others, but to honor Him. This doesn't mean perfection. It means doing our best with what we've been given, in a spirit of worship.

DEVOTIONAL THOUGHT

Perfectionism paralyzes, but excellence inspires. When we pursue excellence, we reflect God's nature—orderly, creative, and intentional. But when we chase perfection, we're often chasing approval. God doesn't require flawless work—He desires faithful stewardship.

APPLICATION

Where has perfectionism held you back? This week, aim for excellence—doing your best, finishing what you start, and improving where you can. But release the need to please everyone. Let your standard be faithfulness, not flawlessness. Remember, for those looking to launch, it doesn't need to be perfect to get started.

REFLECTION

Where are you striving for perfection instead of pursuing excellence before God?

PRAYER

Lord,

Thank You that You don't expect perfection from me. I commit to serve You with excellence—not to impress, but to honor. Give me peace in progress and joy in the journey.

Amen.

SCRIPTURE FOCUS

COLOSSIANS 3:23 – "Whatever you do, work at it with all your heart, as working for the Lord, not for human masters."
What part of this week's verse stood out to you the most?

_____

_____

_____

MAIN INSIGHT OR TAKEAWAY

What truth or lesson did God highlight for you through the devotional?

_____

_____

_____

PERSONAL APPLICATION

How will you apply this to your business or leadership this week?

_____

_____

_____

CHALLENGES OR CONVICTIONS

Did anything convict, challenge, or stretch you?

_____

_____

_____

ANSWERED PRAYERS / PRAISE REPORT

Did you see God show up in any way this week?

_____

_____

_____

PRAYER FOR THE WEEK

Write a personal prayer based on your reflection.

_____

_____

_____

NEXT STEP OR ACTION ITEM

What's one specific action you'll take based on this reflection?

_____

_____

_____

VERSE

MARK 6:31 – *"Then, because so many people were coming and going that they did not even have a chance to eat, He said to them, 'Come with me by yourselves to a quiet place and get some rest.'"*

INTERPRETATION

Even Jesus pulled away from the crowds. He invited His disciples to rest when things were busiest—not because there was nothing to do, but because their souls needed room to breathe.

DEVOTIONAL THOUGHT

Margin is the space between your limits and your load. Without it, stress builds, creativity dies, and burnout looms. God doesn't want you running on empty. He wants you to build rhythms that honor your human design—and His divine wisdom.

APPLICATION

Review your calendar. Where can you protect some margin? Block time for rest, reflection, or simply being present. Don't wait for an emergency to force you into stillness. Make space now, and let God refresh your perspective. This is truly where you will find this so called 'BALANCE'

REFLECTION

What's one boundary you can set this week to create more margin in your schedule? Learn how to turn off the world and just be...

PRAYER

Father,
Thank You for modeling rest and rhythm.
Teach me to build margin into my days and
how to use it so I can hear Your voice, restore
my soul, and lead from a healthy place.
Amen.

WEEK 18

SCRIPTURE FOCUS

MARK 6:31 – "Then, because so many people were coming and going that they did not even have a chance to eat, He said to them, 'Come with me by yourselves to a quiet place and get some rest.'"

What part of this week's verse stood out to you the most?

MAIN INSIGHT OR TAKEAWAY

What truth or lesson did God highlight for you through the devotional?

PERSONAL APPLICATION

How will you apply this to your business or leadership this week?

CHALLENGES OR CONVICTIONS

Did anything convict, challenge, or stretch you?

ANSWERED PRAYERS / PRAISE REPORT

Did you see God show up in any way this week?

PRAYER FOR THE WEEK

Write a personal prayer based on your reflection.

NEXT STEP OR ACTION ITEM

What's one specific action you'll take based on this reflection?

VERSE

PHILIPPIANS 4:19 – *"And my God will meet all your needs according to the riches of His glory in Christ Jesus."*

INTERPRETATION:

Clients, contracts, or cash flow may be the channels, but they are not the source. God is your Provider, and His resources are limitless. When we rely on Him first, we operate from peace instead of panic.

DEVOTIONAL THOUGHT:

In business, it's easy to tie your peace to revenue. But when you remember that God—not your circumstances—is your source, fear loses its grip. He sees what you need and when you need it. His provision often comes in unexpected ways, but it always comes with purpose.

APPLICATION:

This week, practice speaking faith over your finances and decisions. If you're in a season of tightness, replace worry with worship. Ask God to provide—and expect Him to move, even if it's not in the way you imagined.

REFLECTION:

Are you looking to a person, system, or account as your source instead of God? What habits can you add this week to bring yourself closer to understanding that your business partner, God, is supporting your efforts?

PRAYER:

Jehovah Jireh,
You are my Provider. I trust You—not just for what I need today, but for what You see coming tomorrow. Remind me that You are my source, and everything else is simply a vessel in Your hands. Amen.

WEEK 19

SCRIPTURE FOCUS
PHILIPPIANS 4:19 – "And my God will meet all your needs according to the riches of His glory in Christ Jesus."
What part of this week's verse stood out to you the most?

MAIN INSIGHT OR TAKEAWAY
What truth or lesson did God highlight for you through the devotional?

PERSONAL APPLICATION
How will you apply this to your business or leadership this week?

CHALLENGES OR CONVICTIONS
Did anything convict, challenge, or stretch you?

ANSWERED PRAYERS / PRAISE REPORT
Did you see God show up in any way this week?

PRAYER FOR THE WEEK
Write a personal prayer based on your reflection.

NEXT STEP OR ACTION ITEM
What's one specific action you'll take based on this reflection?

VERSE

JOSHUA 1:9 – *"Have I not commanded you? Be strong and courageous. Do not be afraid; do not be discouraged, for the Lord your God will be with you wherever you go."*

INTERPRETATION

God commands courage not because we're fearless, but because He's with us. The presence of God is what empowers us to move forward—even when the next step feels uncertain.

DEVOTIONAL THOUGHT

Every business owner hits moments of hesitation—launching something new, hiring someone, letting go of what no longer works. Fear whispers, "What if it fails?" God's voice says, "I'm with you." Courage doesn't mean the absence of fear—it means obedience in the presence of it.

APPLICATION

What's your next bold move? Write it down. Then pray for God's courage to take the first small step this week. You don't have to see the whole path—just obey the next thing.

REFLECTION

What decision have you been delaying because of fear? What can you do to move past this delay?

PRAYER

God,

You have not called me to play it safe. Thank You for the courage to act on what You've placed in my heart. I know that You go before me and stand beside me. I commit to move forward in obedience, not fear.

Amen.

39

SCRIPTURE FOCUS

JOSHUA 1:9 – "Have I not commanded you? Be strong and courageous. Do not be afraid; do not be discouraged, for the Lord your God will be with you wherever you go."

What part of this week's verse stood out to you the most?

_____

_____

MAIN INSIGHT OR TAKEAWAY

What truth or lesson did God highlight for you through the devotional?

_____

_____

_____

PERSONAL APPLICATION

How will you apply this to your business or leadership this week?

_____

_____

_____

CHALLENGES OR CONVICTIONS

Did anything convict, challenge, or stretch you?

_____

_____

_____

ANSWERED PRAYERS / PRAISE REPORT

Did you see God show up in any way this week?

_____

_____

_____

PRAYER FOR THE WEEK

Write a personal prayer based on your reflection.

_____

_____

_____

NEXT STEP OR ACTION ITEM

What's one specific action you'll take based on this reflection?

_____

_____

_____

VERSE

PROVERBS 13:20 — *"Walk with the wise and become wise, for a companion of fools suffers harm."*

INTERPRETATION

The people you surround yourself with will shape your decisions, direction, and ultimately your destiny. Godly counsel multiplies wisdom. Careless company multiplies compromise.

DEVOTIONAL THOUGHT

Entrepreneurship can feel isolating—but you weren't meant to do this alone. The right people will sharpen you, support you, and call you higher. Don't just network. Build relationships with those who carry Kingdom values and character.

APPLICATION

Take inventory of your inner circle—advisors, peers, mentors. Are they pushing you closer to God's best, or pulling you into compromise? This week, seek out one wise person and invite their insight into a current challenge.

REFLECTION

Who in your life sharpens you spiritually and professionally—and who might need some distance?

PRAYER

Lord,
Surround me with people who speak truth, live with integrity, and reflect Your heart. I commit to walk with the wise so I can grow in both faith and leadership. Give me discernment about who I allow to influence my journey.
Amen.

WEEK 21

SCRIPTURE FOCUS
PROVERBS 13:20 – "Walk with the wise and become wise, for a companion of fools suffers harm."
What part of this week's verse stood out to you the most?

_____
_____
_____

MAIN INSIGHT OR TAKEAWAY
What truth or lesson did God highlight for you through the devotional?

_____
_____
_____

PERSONAL APPLICATION
How will you apply this to your business or leadership this week?

_____
_____
_____

CHALLENGES OR CONVICTIONS
Did anything convict, challenge, or stretch you?

_____
_____
_____

ANSWERED PRAYERS / PRAISE REPORT
Did you see God show up in any way this week?

_____
_____
_____

PRAYER FOR THE WEEK
Write a personal prayer based on your reflection.

_____
_____
_____

NEXT STEP OR ACTION ITEM
What's one specific action you'll take based on this reflection?

_____
_____
_____

VERSE

PHILIPPIANS 2:3 – *"Do nothing out of selfish ambition or vain conceit. Rather, in humility valuing others above yourselves."*

INTERPRETATION

Kingdom leadership isn't built on ego, but on humility. True influence comes from lifting others up, not climbing over them. God exalts the humble and resists the proud.

DEVOTIONAL THOUGHT

In business, success can easily feed pride. But Jesus modeled a different way—He washed feet, served others, and led with love. Humility doesn't mean weakness; it means knowing who you are in God and using your strength to benefit others.

APPLICATION

Look for ways to lead with humility this week. Celebrate your team. Admit a mistake. Ask for input. Shift the spotlight. Humble leadership builds trust and honors God.

REFLECTION

Where might pride be creeping in, and how can you choose humility instead? Keep up with an accountability partner who will help you identify the times where you struggle to remain humble.

PRAYER

Jesus,

You led with humility, even when You had every reason to claim glory. I commit to lead like You—serving others, listening well, and staying grounded in grace. Keep my heart soft and my posture low.

Amen.

WEEK 22

SCRIPTURE FOCUS

PHILIPPIANS 2:3 – "Do nothing out of selfish ambition or vain conceit. Rather, in humility valuing others above yourselves."

What part of this week's verse stood out to you the most?

_____

_____

MAIN INSIGHT OR TAKEAWAY

What truth or lesson did God highlight for you through the devotional?

_____

_____

_____

PERSONAL APPLICATION

How will you apply this to your business or leadership this week?

_____

_____

_____

CHALLENGES OR CONVICTIONS

Did anything convict, challenge, or stretch you?

_____

_____

_____

ANSWERED PRAYERS / PRAISE REPORT

Did you see God show up in any way this week?

_____

_____

_____

PRAYER FOR THE WEEK

Write a personal prayer based on your reflection.

_____

_____

_____

NEXT STEP OR ACTION ITEM

What's one specific action you'll take based on this reflection?

_____

_____

_____

VERSE

PSALM 34:18 – *"The Lord is close to the brokenhearted and saves those who are crushed in spirit."*

INTERPRETATION

God doesn't avoid our disappointment—He draws near to it. When our expectations aren't met, He offers comfort and renewal. He sees what's lost and promises redemption.

DEVOTIONAL THOUGHT

Business comes with highs and lows. Not every launch goes well. Not every deal closes. Disappointment can make you question your calling. But God sees the full picture. He uses even what feels like failure to shape you and redirect you into something better.

APPLICATION

Acknowledge your disappointments honestly with God. Don't minimize or ignore them. Instead, hand them over and ask what He wants to do through them. Let Him heal your heart and restore your hope.

REFLECTION

What business setback do you need to receive honestly and surrender to God?

PRAYER

Father,

You know my heart and my hopes. You see what hasn't worked and what still hurts. I invite You into my disappointment. Redeem it. Use it. And renew my trust in You, even when the outcome isn't what I expected.

Amen.

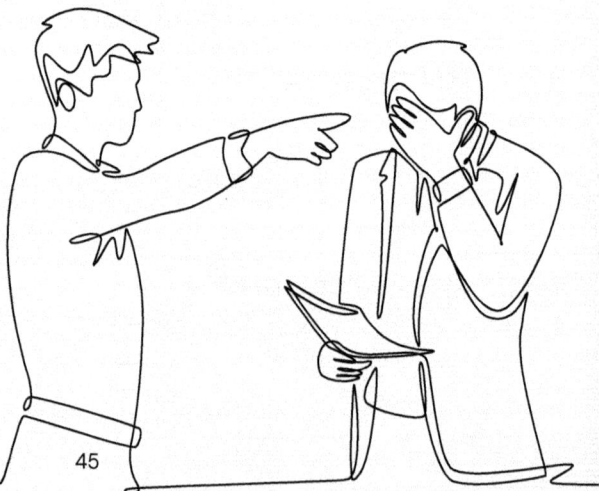

SCRIPTURE FOCUS

PSALM 34:18 – "The Lord is close to the brokenhearted and saves those who are crushed in spirit."

What part of this week's verse stood out to you the most?

_____
_____
_____

MAIN INSIGHT OR TAKEAWAY

What truth or lesson did God highlight for you through the devotional?

_____
_____
_____

PERSONAL APPLICATION

How will you apply this to your business or leadership this week?

_____
_____
_____

CHALLENGES OR CONVICTIONS

Did anything convict, challenge, or stretch you?

_____
_____
_____

ANSWERED PRAYERS / PRAISE REPORT

Did you see God show up in any way this week?

_____
_____
_____

PRAYER FOR THE WEEK

Write a personal prayer based on your reflection.

_____
_____
_____

NEXT STEP OR ACTION ITEM

What's one specific action you'll take based on this reflection?

_____
_____
_____

VERSE

MATTHEW 25:23 — *"Well done, good and faithful servant! You have been faithful with a few things; I will put you in charge of many things."*

INTERPRETATION

God honors faithfulness, not just visibility. While the world applauds popularity and scale, God rewards consistent obedience and quiet excellence.

DEVOTIONAL THOUGHT

It's easy to crave "the big break" or viral success. But the most impactful businesses are built through daily diligence and unseen sacrifice. God sees what no one else does. Your faithful work, done with integrity, honors Him deeply—no matter who's watching.

APPLICATION

Instead of trying to impress this week, focus on being faithful. Do the next right thing with care. Follow through. Be consistent in the small. Let God handle the increase.

REFLECTION

What area of your business needs a renewed commitment to daily faithfulness?

PRAYER

God,
I want to hear "well done" from You—not just applause from others.
I commit to staying faithful in the little things. Teach me to be steady, consistent, and committed, knowing that You see it all and will reward it in due time.
Amen.

WEEK 24

SCRIPTURE FOCUS

MATTHEW 25:23 – "Well done, good and faithful servant! You have been faithful with a few things; I will put you in charge of many things."

What part of this week's verse stood out to you the most?

_____

_____

MAIN INSIGHT OR TAKEAWAY

What truth or lesson did God highlight for you through the devotional?

_____

_____

_____

PERSONAL APPLICATION

How will you apply this to your business or leadership this week?

_____

_____

_____

CHALLENGES OR CONVICTIONS

Did anything convict, challenge, or stretch you?

_____

_____

_____

ANSWERED PRAYERS / PRAISE REPORT

Did you see God show up in any way this week?

_____

_____

_____

PRAYER FOR THE WEEK

Write a personal prayer based on your reflection.

_____

_____

_____

NEXT STEP OR ACTION ITEM

What's one specific action you'll take based on this reflection?

_____

_____

VERSE

ISAIAH 40:31 – *"But those who hope in the Lord will renew their strength. They will soar on wings like eagles; they will run and not grow weary, they will walk and not be faint."*

INTERPRETATION

Waiting on God is not passive—it's an act of trust. When we place our hope in Him instead of outcomes, He renews our strength and gives us vision beyond the delay.

DEVOTIONAL THOUGHT

Waiting seasons in business can feel like wasted time. But God often does His deepest work while we wait. He strengthens your spirit, refines your motives, and prepares opportunities behind the scenes. You're not stuck—you're being shaped.

APPLICATION

Where are you waiting in your business—on growth, clarity, finances, or breakthrough? This week, choose to wait with God instead of just waiting on Him. Use the time to prepare your heart, sharpen your skills, and renew your trust.

REFLECTION

How can you turn your waiting into worship and preparation? Is there one area you believe is in the 'waiting season' that you want to pray over for clarity?

PRAYER

Lord,
Waiting is hard, but I know You never
waste it. Strengthen me in the stillness.
I trust Your timing and look forward to
what You are already preparing for me.
Amen.

SCRIPTURE FOCUS

ISAIAH 40:31 – "But those who hope in the Lord will renew their strength. They will soar on wings like eagles; they will run and not grow weary, they will walk and not be faint."

What part of this week's verse stood out to you the most?

MAIN INSIGHT OR TAKEAWAY

What truth or lesson did God highlight for you through the devotional?

PERSONAL APPLICATION

How will you apply this to your business or leadership this week?

CHALLENGES OR CONVICTIONS

Did anything convict, challenge, or stretch you?

ANSWERED PRAYERS / PRAISE REPORT

Did you see God show up in any way this week?

PRAYER FOR THE WEEK

Write a personal prayer based on your reflection.

NEXT STEP OR ACTION ITEM

What's one specific action you'll take based on this reflection?

VERSE

ROMANS 12:10 – *"Be devoted to one another in love. Honor one another above yourselves."*

INTERPRETATION

Honor means seeing others the way God sees them and treating them with respect, even when it's not earned. A culture of honor reflects God's Kingdom and draws out the best in people.

DEVOTIONAL THOUGHT

Your business culture is shaped by what you celebrate, tolerate, and communicate. Honor builds trust, boosts morale, and makes people feel valued. Whether you're leading one or many, choosing to honor others—employees, clients, or partners—transforms your influence.

APPLICATION

Speak words of appreciation this week. Publicly affirm someone's contribution. Correct with grace. Set the tone that everyone is valued—not just for what they do, but for who they are.

REFLECTION

What's one relationship or environment where you can intentionally show honor this week?

PRAYER

Father,
I commit to lead with honor. Let my words and actions reflect Your love. Teach me to see others as You do and create an atmosphere where people feel seen, respected, and empowered. Teach me to understand when to separate with dignity as well so I do not allow myself to dishonor through delay or dishonesty.
Amen.

SCRIPTURE FOCUS

ROMANS 12:10 – "Be devoted to one another in love. Honor one another above yourselves."
What part of this week's verse stood out to you the most?

_____

_____

_____

MAIN INSIGHT OR TAKEAWAY

What truth or lesson did God highlight for you through the devotional?

_____

_____

_____

PERSONAL APPLICATION

How will you apply this to your business or leadership this week?

_____

_____

_____

CHALLENGES OR CONVICTIONS

Did anything convict, challenge, or stretch you?

_____

_____

_____

ANSWERED PRAYERS / PRAISE REPORT

Did you see God show up in any way this week?

_____

_____

_____

PRAYER FOR THE WEEK

Write a personal prayer based on your reflection.

_____

_____

_____

NEXT STEP OR ACTION ITEM

What's one specific action you'll take based on this reflection?

_____

_____

_____

VERSE

PROVERBS 3:5–6 – *Trust in the Lord with all your heart and lean not on your own understanding; in all your ways submit to Him, and He will make your paths straight."*

INTERPRETATION

God doesn't ask us to control outcomes—He asks us to trust Him through the process. Submitting to His wisdom means releasing our obsession with results and walking in obedience.

DEVOTIONAL THOUGHT

We often equate success with numbers, recognition, or expansion. But in God's economy, success is about obedience. He calls you to sow faithfully, work diligently, and trust that He's working all things together—even when the results don't show up right away.

APPLICATION

Think of one area in your business where you're trying to force results. This week, shift your focus from controlling the outcome to honoring the process. Let faith lead your planning, not fear.

REFLECTION

What part of your business are you holding too tightly instead of entrusting it to God?

PRAYER

God,

I release the outcomes I've been trying to control. I choose to walk in trust and obedience, knowing that You direct my steps and work all things together for good.

Amen.

SCRIPTURE FOCUS

PROVERBS 3:5–6 — Trust in the Lord with all your heart and lean not on your own understanding; in all your ways submit to Him, and He will make your paths straight."

What part of this week's verse stood out to you the most?

_____

_____

MAIN INSIGHT OR TAKEAWAY

What truth or lesson did God highlight for you through the devotional?

_____

_____

_____

PERSONAL APPLICATION

How will you apply this to your business or leadership this week?

_____

_____

_____

CHALLENGES OR CONVICTIONS

Did anything convict, challenge, or stretch you?

_____

_____

_____

ANSWERED PRAYERS / PRAISE REPORT

Did you see God show up in any way this week?

_____

_____

_____

PRAYER FOR THE WEEK

Write a personal prayer based on your reflection.

_____

_____

_____

NEXT STEP OR ACTION ITEM

What's one specific action you'll take based on this reflection?

_____

_____

_____

VERSE

LUKE 16:10 – *"Whoever can be trusted with very little can also be trusted with much, and whoever is dishonest with very little will also be dishonest with much."*

INTERPRETATION

God watches how we steward both the large and small responsibilities. He is not impressed by scale—He is moved by character. Faithfulness in little things prepares us for greater responsibility.

DEVOTIONAL THOUGHT

The world may not notice the corners you refuse to cut or the quiet choices to do what's right. But God sees. Integrity in your business practices—contracts, payroll, reporting, and relationships—builds a foundation God can bless.

APPLICATION

Choose one area of your business this week where you can strengthen integrity. Whether it's how you invoice, how you speak about a competitor, or how you treat your team—be faithful in the details.

REFLECTION

Where might small compromises be creeping in, and how can you honor God instead? Look for areas where you may have taken shortcuts that decreased your quality or integrity in your offerings.

PRAYER

God of truth,
I commit to being trustworthy in the small things. Keep my heart aligned with Your values and release within me the courage to choose integrity over convenience. Let my business reflect honesty at every level.
Amen.

SCRIPTURE FOCUS

LUKE 16:10 – "Whoever can be trusted with very little can also be trusted with much, and whoever is dishonest with very little will also be dishonest with much."

What part of this week's verse stood out to you the most?

MAIN INSIGHT OR TAKEAWAY

What truth or lesson did God highlight for you through the devotional?

PERSONAL APPLICATION

How will you apply this to your business or leadership this week?

CHALLENGES OR CONVICTIONS

Did anything convict, challenge, or stretch you?

ANSWERED PRAYERS / PRAISE REPORT

Did you see God show up in any way this week?

PRAYER FOR THE WEEK

Write a personal prayer based on your reflection.

NEXT STEP OR ACTION ITEM

What's one specific action you'll take based on this reflection?

VERSE

PSALM 37:23–24 – *"The Lord makes firm the steps of the one who delights in Him; though he may stumble, he will not fall, for the Lord upholds him with His hand."*

INTERPRETATION

Stuck seasons do not mean God has left you. Even when movement is slow or unclear, He is ordering your steps. Your foundation is secure in Him.

DEVOTIONAL THOUGHT

Business momentum isn't always constant. There are seasons when decisions stall, growth plateaus, or clarity fades. In those moments, don't panic—press in. God often does deep work in stillness. Trust He is guiding even your pauses.

APPLICATION

Resist the urge to force progress this week. Instead, seek God in prayer and reflection. Ask, "What are You teaching me here?" Your next step may not be action—but surrender. Are you really ready for what's to come?

REFLECTION

What's one area of your business that feels stuck—and how might God be using it?

PRAYER

Lord,
When I feel stuck, remind me that You are still with me. Make my heart sensitive to Your direction and release the patience You've provided to wait on You. I trust and operate in the pace You've set.
Amen.

57

SCRIPTURE FOCUS

PSALM 37:23–24 – "The Lord makes firm the steps of the one who delights in Him; though he may stumble, he will not fall, for the Lord upholds him with His hand."

What part of this week's verse stood out to you the most?

_____

_____

MAIN INSIGHT OR TAKEAWAY

What truth or lesson did God highlight for you through the devotional?

_____

_____

_____

PERSONAL APPLICATION

How will you apply this to your business or leadership this week?

_____

_____

_____

CHALLENGES OR CONVICTIONS

Did anything convict, challenge, or stretch you?

_____

_____

_____

ANSWERED PRAYERS / PRAISE REPORT

Did you see God show up in any way this week?

_____

_____

_____

PRAYER FOR THE WEEK

Write a personal prayer based on your reflection.

_____

_____

_____

NEXT STEP OR ACTION ITEM

What's one specific action you'll take based on this reflection?

_____

_____

_____

VERSE

MATTHEW 6:33 – *"But seek first His kingdom and His righteousness, and all these things will be given to you as well."*

INTERPRETATION

When God's Kingdom is your first pursuit, everything else—provision, growth, peace—falls into place in alignment with His will.

DEVOTIONAL THOUGHT

In business, we often measure success by profit, reach, or reviews. But Kingdom success is measured by obedience, impact, and transformation. When you seek God's will first, even your metrics shift.

APPLICATION

Reevaluate your goals this week. Are they Kingdom-aligned or just performance-based? Choose one goal to reframe through the lens of honoring God and serving people.

REFLECTION

Are your current business goals rooted in God's priorities—or in pressure to perform?

PRAYER

Father,
Refocus my vision. Let me seek first Your Kingdom, not just growth or gain. I choose to set goals that please You and pursue success that honors You.
Amen.

WEEK 30

SCRIPTURE FOCUS
MATTHEW 6:33 – "But seek first His kingdom and His righteousness, and all these things will be given to you as well."
What part of this week's verse stood out to you the most?

_____
_____
_____

MAIN INSIGHT OR TAKEAWAY
What truth or lesson did God highlight for you through the devotional?

_____
_____
_____

PERSONAL APPLICATION
How will you apply this to your business or leadership this week?

_____
_____
_____

CHALLENGES OR CONVICTIONS
Did anything convict, challenge, or stretch you?

_____
_____
_____

ANSWERED PRAYERS / PRAISE REPORT
Did you see God show up in any way this week?

_____
_____
_____

PRAYER FOR THE WEEK
Write a personal prayer based on your reflection.

_____
_____
_____

NEXT STEP OR ACTION ITEM
What's one specific action you'll take based on this reflection?

_____
_____
_____

VERSE

HEBREWS 10:24– *"And let us consider how we may spur one another on toward love and good deeds."*

INTERPRETATION

God calls us to be encouragers—people who build up, inspire, and strengthen others. In a competitive world, encouragement is a powerful Kingdom tool.

DEVOTIONAL THOUGHT

As leaders, we can be so focused on productivity that we forget the power of our words. A timely encouragement can change someone's week—or life. Encouragement doesn't cost anything, but it yields eternal results.

APPLICATION

Intentionally encourage someone this week—a team member, a peer, a vendor, or even a competitor. Speak life into their calling.

REFLECTION

Who in your business world needs encouragement right now? Who is encouraging you?

PRAYER

God,

Make me an encourager. I choose to see people the way You see them. Let my words lift others up and create a culture of support and strength.

Amen.

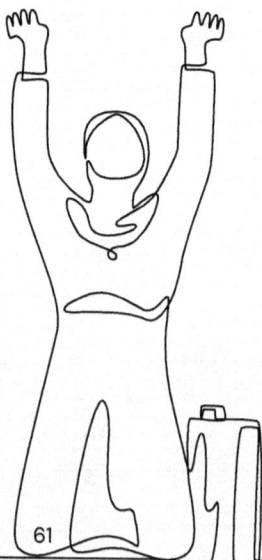

SCRIPTURE FOCUS

HEBREWS 10:24– "And let us consider how we may spur one another on toward love and good deeds."
What part of this week's verse stood out to you the most?

_____
_____
_____

MAIN INSIGHT OR TAKEAWAY

What truth or lesson did God highlight for you through the devotional?

_____
_____
_____

PERSONAL APPLICATION

How will you apply this to your business or leadership this week?

_____
_____
_____

CHALLENGES OR CONVICTIONS

Did anything convict, challenge, or stretch you?

_____
_____
_____

ANSWERED PRAYERS / PRAISE REPORT

Did you see God show up in any way this week?

_____
_____
_____

PRAYER FOR THE WEEK

Write a personal prayer based on your reflection.

_____
_____
_____

NEXT STEP OR ACTION ITEM

What's one specific action you'll take based on this reflection?

_____
_____
_____

VERSE

ROMANS 5:3–4 (ESV) *"Not only that, but we rejoice in our sufferings, knowing that suffering produces endurance, and endurance produces character, and character produces hope."*

INTERPRETATION

Paul reminds us that suffering is not the end of the story—it is part of a divine process. God uses difficulty to cultivate in us endurance, character, and hope. As entrepreneurs and small business leaders, we will inevitably face trials. But these trials are purposeful and refining.

DEVOTIONAL THOUGHT

In the business world, hardship is often viewed as failure. But God's Word shows us that hardship is fertile ground for spiritual growth, perseverance, and long-term hope. When we shift our mindset from despair to rejoicing, we align our hearts with God's greater purpose.

APPLICATION

When a deal falls through, a key client leaves, or we face financial pressure, we can choose to respond in faith, not fear. Use adversity as an opportunity to develop stronger leadership muscles, greater prayer habits, and deeper trust in God's timing. Share the journey transparently with your team—modeling faith during difficulty is one of the most powerful forms of leadership.

REFLECTION

What recent challenge in your business has God used to develop your endurance? Are you more focused on escaping discomfort or on growing through it? How can you build a culture in your business that views challenges through the lens of faith and hope?

PRAYER

Lord,

Help me not to fear suffering, but to rejoice in it knowing You are working behind the scenes to strengthen me. Grow my endurance and shape my character so that my hope in You shines even brighter. May every trial lead me closer to You and become a testimony of Your faithfulness in my life and business. Amen.

SCRIPTURE FOCUS

ROMANS 5:3–4 (ESV) "Not only that, but we rejoice in our sufferings, knowing that suffering produces endurance, and endurance produces character, and character produces hope."

What part of this week's verse stood out to you the most?

_____

_____

MAIN INSIGHT OR TAKEAWAY

What truth or lesson did God highlight for you through the devotional?

_____

_____

_____

PERSONAL APPLICATION

How will you apply this to your business or leadership this week?

_____

_____

_____

CHALLENGES OR CONVICTIONS

Did anything convict, challenge, or stretch you?

_____

_____

_____

ANSWERED PRAYERS / PRAISE REPORT

Did you see God show up in any way this week?

_____

_____

_____

PRAYER FOR THE WEEK

Write a personal prayer based on your reflection.

_____

_____

_____

NEXT STEP OR ACTION ITEM

What's one specific action you'll take based on this reflection?

_____

_____

_____

VERSE

GALATIANS 6:9– *"Let us not become weary in doing good, for at the proper time we will reap a harvest if we do not give up."*

INTERPRETATION

God sees the good you do, even when no one else does. His rewards come in the right time—not always on your timeline, but always on His.

DEVOTIONAL THOUGHT

It's hard to keep showing up when no one notices. But God notices. He honors your faithfulness in the hidden places. Keep sowing, keep serving, and keep trusting that your harvest is coming. Entrepreneurship is a lonely place. Remember to include God in the process.

APPLICATION

Stay faithful in a hard place this week. Do the right thing—even if no one applauds. God sees you.

REFLECTION

Where have you been sowing without seeing fruit—and how can you stay encouraged?

PRAYER

Father,
I will not grow weary in doing good. Thank you that You see my faithfulness and that my labor in You is never wasted. Your strength keeps me going. Help me to accept my knowledge of your partnership as enough without the need for recognition from this world.
Amen.

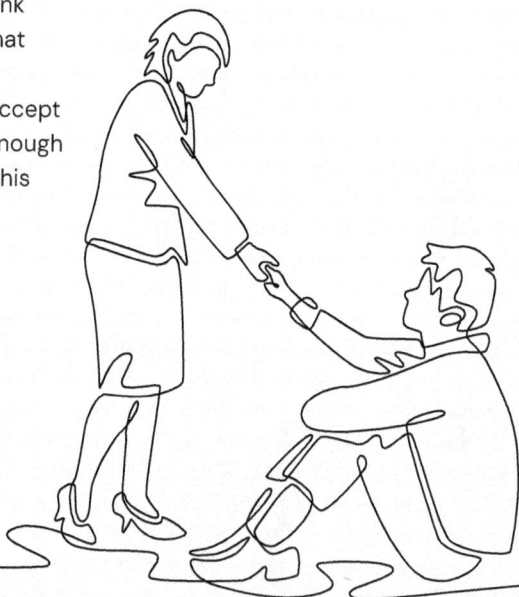

SCRIPTURE FOCUS

GALATIANS 6:9– "Let us not become weary in doing good, for at the proper time we will reap a harvest if we do not give up."

What part of this week's verse stood out to you the most?

_____

_____

MAIN INSIGHT OR TAKEAWAY

What truth or lesson did God highlight for you through the devotional?

_____

_____

_____

PERSONAL APPLICATION

How will you apply this to your business or leadership this week?

_____

_____

_____

CHALLENGES OR CONVICTIONS

Did anything convict, challenge, or stretch you?

_____

_____

_____

ANSWERED PRAYERS / PRAISE REPORT

Did you see God show up in any way this week?

_____

_____

_____

PRAYER FOR THE WEEK

Write a personal prayer based on your reflection.

_____

_____

_____

NEXT STEP OR ACTION ITEM

What's one specific action you'll take based on this reflection?

_____

_____

_____

VERSE

PROVERBS 4:23– *"Above all else, guard your heart, for everything you do flows from it."*

INTERPRETATION

Boundaries protect what matters most. Your heart—your motives, energy, peace—requires guarding so that your work and relationships remain healthy and Spirit-led.

DEVOTIONAL THOUGHT

In business, the lines between hustle and health can blur. Setting boundaries isn't weakness—it's wisdom. Boundaries help you serve others without losing yourself, rest without guilt, and lead without burnout.

APPLICATION

Identify one boundary you need to (re)establish this week—whether it's around time, communication, or expectations. Guard your heart so you can lead from a place of wholeness.

REFLECTION

What boundary do you need to reinforce in order to protect your peace? What difficult discussions might you need to have?

PRAYER

God,
Show me where I need better boundaries. I purpose to guard my heart and lead with wisdom. Give me courage to say no when needed so I can say yes to what truly matters.
Amen.

WEEK 34

SCRIPTURE FOCUS
PROVERBS 4:23– "Above all else, guard your heart, for everything you do flows from it."
What part of this week's verse stood out to you the most?

_____
_____
_____

MAIN INSIGHT OR TAKEAWAY
What truth or lesson did God highlight for you through the devotional?

_____
_____
_____

PERSONAL APPLICATION
How will you apply this to your business or leadership this week?

_____
_____
_____

CHALLENGES OR CONVICTIONS
Did anything convict, challenge, or stretch you?

_____
_____
_____

ANSWERED PRAYERS / PRAISE REPORT
Did you see God show up in any way this week?

_____
_____
_____

PRAYER FOR THE WEEK
Write a personal prayer based on your reflection.

_____
_____
_____

NEXT STEP OR ACTION ITEM
What's one specific action you'll take based on this reflection?

_____
_____
_____

VERSE

ECCLESIASTES 3:11 – *"He has made everything beautiful in its time."*

INTERPRETATION

God operates on a divine timeline that often doesn't match our own. He is not rushed or delayed. What He brings forth in His timing carries lasting beauty and purpose.

DEVOTIONAL THOUGHT

In entrepreneurship, we want things to happen fast—launches, growth, deals. But impatience can lead to missteps. Trust that God's delay is not denial. He's preparing you and others for the right moment and be prepared to receive.

APPLICATION

Practice patience this week. If a door hasn't opened yet, don't force it. Use the waiting time to prepare, reflect, and strengthen your faith.

REFLECTION

What are you waiting on, and how can you better trust God's timing? Are you watching for answers that are different then what you expected or wanted them to be, so are thinking that there is a delay that is not there?

PRAYER

Lord,

Thank You for working in perfect timing. Teach me to wait with expectation and faith. I rest in knowing You are never late and you will keep me safe from mistakes.

Amen.

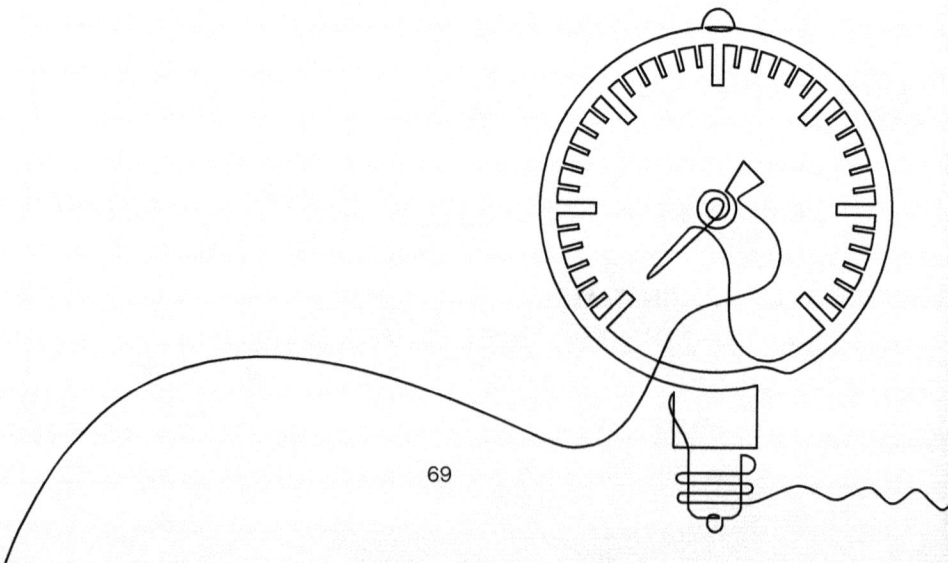

SCRIPTURE FOCUS

ECCLESIASTES 3:11 – "He has made everything beautiful in its time."
What part of this week's verse stood out to you the most?

_____
_____
_____

MAIN INSIGHT OR TAKEAWAY

What truth or lesson did God highlight for you through the devotional?

_____
_____
_____

PERSONAL APPLICATION

How will you apply this to your business or leadership this week?

_____
_____
_____

CHALLENGES OR CONVICTIONS

Did anything convict, challenge, or stretch you?

_____
_____
_____

ANSWERED PRAYERS / PRAISE REPORT

Did you see God show up in any way this week?

_____
_____
_____

PRAYER FOR THE WEEK

Write a personal prayer based on your reflection.

_____
_____
_____

NEXT STEP OR ACTION ITEM

What's one specific action you'll take based on this reflection?

_____
_____
_____

VERSE

1 PETER 4:10 – *"Each of you should use whatever gift you have received to serve others, as faithful stewards of God's grace in its various forms."*

INTERPRETATION

Your skills, passions, and resources are not just for your benefit. They are entrusted to you to bless and serve others.

DEVOTIONAL THOUGHT

Entrepreneurship is an opportunity to steward your God-given talents. Whether it's creativity, strategy, leadership, or service—your gifts are part of God's plan to impact the world.

APPLICATION

Identify a gift or strength and ask, "How can I use this to serve someone today?" Shift your focus from profit to purpose.

REFLECTION

Are you using your gifts to glorify God or merely to advance yourself? Do you have a clear understanding of God's purpose for your life through service?

PRAYER

Father,

Thank You for the gifts You've entrusted to me. I will steward them well and use them to serve others with joy and humility. I will be on the constant pursuit of living the purpose you have provided to me with clarity and partnership with you.

Amen.

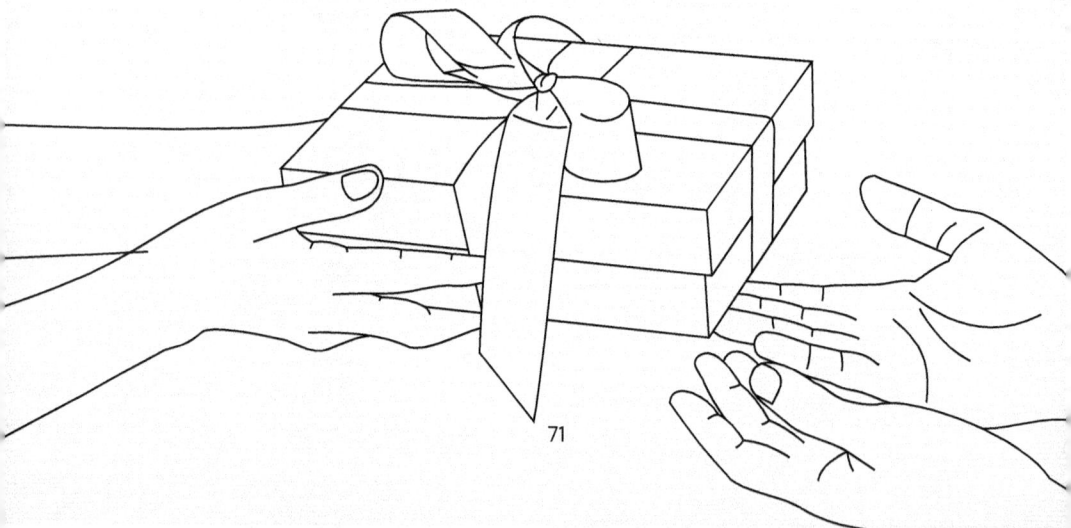

SCRIPTURE FOCUS

1 PETER 4:10 – "Each of you should use whatever gift you have received to serve others, as faithful stewards of God's grace in its various forms."

What part of this week's verse stood out to you the most?

_____

_____

MAIN INSIGHT OR TAKEAWAY

What truth or lesson did God highlight for you through the devotional?

_____

_____

_____

PERSONAL APPLICATION

How will you apply this to your business or leadership this week?

_____

_____

_____

CHALLENGES OR CONVICTIONS

Did anything convict, challenge, or stretch you?

_____

_____

_____

ANSWERED PRAYERS / PRAISE REPORT

Did you see God show up in any way this week?

_____

_____

_____

PRAYER FOR THE WEEK

Write a personal prayer based on your reflection.

_____

_____

_____

NEXT STEP OR ACTION ITEM

What's one specific action you'll take based on this reflection?

_____

_____

_____

VERSE

PSALM 90:17 (ESV) – *"Let the favor of the Lord our God be upon us, and establish the work of our hands upon us; yes, establish the work of our hands!"*

INTERPRETATION

This verse is a prayer from Moses, asking for God's presence and blessing to rest upon the work he and the people of Israel are doing. It reminds us that no matter how skilled or strategic we are, it is God who ultimately establishes and sustains our work. His favor is what turns our labor into legacy.

DEVOTIONAL THOUGHT

We are called to build with both hands and heart—but only what is built with God's blessing will last. Business is more than strategy; it is stewardship of God's opportunities.

APPLICATION

Begin this and every workweek in prayer, asking God to establish your plans and guide your decisions. Review your current projects and ask: "Am I inviting God into this work, or am I building alone?" Identify areas where you've been striving in your own strength and surrender them to God. Celebrate progress by giving thanks and acknowledging God's hand in every win.

REFLECTION

Where in your business do you need to ask for God's favor and direction? How can you realign your business goals with God's purposes this week?

PRAYER

Father,

Thank You for the work You've placed in my hands. I ask that Your favor would rest on my business and that You would establish the efforts of my heart. Help me to work with diligence and depend on You, not just my own understanding. May everything, I build be a reflection of Your grace and glory.

Amen.

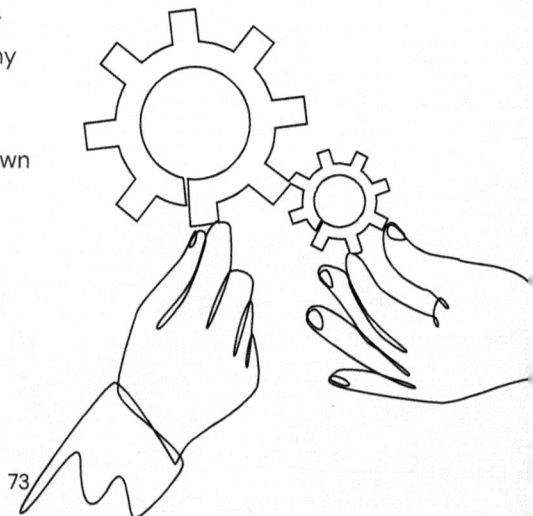

SCRIPTURE FOCUS

90:17 (ESV) – "Let the favor of the Lord our God be upon us, and establish the work of our hands upon us; yes, establish the work of our hands!"

What part of this week's verse stood out to you the most?

_____

_____

MAIN INSIGHT OR TAKEAWAY

What truth or lesson did God highlight for you through the devotional?

_____

_____

_____

PERSONAL APPLICATION

How will you apply this to your business or leadership this week?

_____

_____

_____

CHALLENGES OR CONVICTIONS

Did anything convict, challenge, or stretch you?

_____

_____

_____

ANSWERED PRAYERS / PRAISE REPORT

Did you see God show up in any way this week?

_____

_____

_____

PRAYER FOR THE WEEK

Write a personal prayer based on your reflection.

_____

_____

_____

NEXT STEP OR ACTION ITEM

What's one specific action you'll take based on this reflection?

_____

_____

_____

VERSE

PHILIPPIANS 4:13 (ESV) – *"I can do all things through him who strengthens me."*

INTERPRETATION

This verse is often quoted as a declaration of confidence—but in its full context, it reveals the secret to contentment in both abundance and lack. Paul writes this while imprisoned, reminding us that our true strength comes not from circumstances, skills, or success, but from Christ Himself. He is the source of our endurance, joy, and perseverance in every business challenge we face.

DEVOTIONAL THOUGHT

Your ability to succeed doesn't rest solely on your own abilities. In Christ, you have divine strength to face every demand, difficulty, or doubt that comes your way.

APPLICATION

Start each day by confessing your dependence on God for wisdom and strength. When overwhelmed, remind yourself that Christ is your source—not your hustle, not your network, and not your experience. Teach your team the value of leaning on faith when stress or setbacks come. Keep a "strength list"—ways God has shown up in the past to sustain and provide for you.

REFLECTION

Where do you feel most weak or stretched in your business today? Are you trying to carry your burdens alone, or leaning into God's strength? How will your approach change if you fully believed God is strengthening you?

PRAYER

God,

I confess that I often try to do everything in my own strength. Forgive me for forgetting that You are with me and for me. Help me to rely on You for every task, every meeting, every challenge I face this week. Let Your strength be made perfect in my weakness. Amen.

WEEK 38

SCRIPTURE FOCUS
PHILIPPIANS 4:13 (ESV) – "I can do all things through him who strengthens me."
What part of this week's verse stood out to you the most?

_____
_____
_____

MAIN INSIGHT OR TAKEAWAY
What truth or lesson did God highlight for you through the devotional?

_____
_____
_____

PERSONAL APPLICATION
How will you apply this to your business or leadership this week?

_____
_____
_____

CHALLENGES OR CONVICTIONS
Did anything convict, challenge, or stretch you?

_____
_____
_____

ANSWERED PRAYERS / PRAISE REPORT
Did you see God show up in any way this week?

_____
_____
_____

PRAYER FOR THE WEEK
Write a personal prayer based on your reflection.

_____
_____
_____

NEXT STEP OR ACTION ITEM
What's one specific action you'll take based on this reflection?

_____
_____
_____

VERSE

PROVERBS 28:6 (ESV) – *"Better is a poor man who walks in his integrity than a rich man who is crooked in his ways."*

INTERPRETATION

This verse reminds us that true wealth isn't measured by the size of our profits but by the strength of our character. In a world where cutting corners is often rewarded, God calls us to walk in integrity—regardless of the outcome. He values honest hearts over inflated success.

DEVOTIONAL THOUGHT

Your reputation is a reflection of your integrity. In business, your decisions speak louder than your mission statement. Choose the path that honors God, even when no one else is watching.

APPLICATION

Make honesty and fairness the non-negotiables in all transactions—even when it's costly. When faced with ethical dilemmas, pause and pray before acting. Be transparent with clients, vendors, and staff. Integrity breeds trust, and trust breeds loyalty. Set a tone of accountability throughout your team—what you tolerate becomes culture.

REFLECTION

Have you ever felt pressured to compromise your values to get ahead? Are there areas in your business where integrity has taken a back seat to profit or pressure? What would it look like to re-center your business on godly character this week?

PRAYER

Lord,
I want to walk in integrity, no matter the cost. Help me to choose honesty when it's inconvenient, to speak truth when it's unpopular, and to lead with righteousness when others bend the rules. May my life and business reflect Your character and bring You glory.
Amen.

SCRIPTURE FOCUS

PROVERBS 28:6 (ESV) – "Better is a poor man who walks in his integrity than a rich man who is crooked in his ways."
What part of this week's verse stood out to you the most?

_____
_____
_____

MAIN INSIGHT OR TAKEAWAY

What truth or lesson did God highlight for you through the devotional?

_____
_____
_____

PERSONAL APPLICATION

How will you apply this to your business or leadership this week?

_____
_____
_____

CHALLENGES OR CONVICTIONS

Did anything convict, challenge, or stretch you?

_____
_____
_____

ANSWERED PRAYERS / PRAISE REPORT

Did you see God show up in any way this week?

_____
_____
_____

PRAYER FOR THE WEEK

Write a personal prayer based on your reflection.

_____
_____
_____

NEXT STEP OR ACTION ITEM

What's one specific action you'll take based on this reflection?

_____
_____
_____

VERSE

PSALM 1:3 (ESV) – *"He is like a tree planted by streams of water that yields its fruit in its season, and its leaf does not wither. In all that he does, he prospers."*

INTERPRETATION

This verse paints a vivid picture of the person whose life is rooted in God's Word. Like a tree planted near a constant water source, their growth is steady, their fruit is timely, and their resilience is strong. Prosperity in this context is not quick riches, but a flourishing life that is healthy, productive, and grounded in purpose.

DEVOTIONAL THOUGHT

Lasting success flows from being planted in the right source. Business rooted in God's truth will stand firm through drought and deliver fruit in due season.

APPLICATION

Build a business culture grounded in biblical values like honesty, humility, and stewardship. Prioritize your personal spiritual growth—your business health will often reflect your spiritual health. Stop chasing instant results; instead, nurture long-term fruitfulness by remaining grounded in your mission. Invest in rhythms that keep your "roots" nourished: time in Scripture, prayer, and wise counsel.

REFLECTION

Where are you planted? In the Word of God—or in the noise of the world? Are you seeing fruit in your business? If not, do your roots need deeper nourishment? What season are you in—planting, pruning, or harvesting—and how is God calling you to respond?

PRAYER

Lord,
Help me to be like a tree planted by Your living water. Let my life and business reflect Your steady provision, not unstable striving. May I yield good fruit in the right season and remain grounded in Your truth, even when growth feels slow. I trust You with the timing and the outcome. In Jesus' name, Amen.

WEEK 40

SCRIPTURE FOCUS

PSALM 1:3 (ESV) – "He is like a tree planted by streams of water that yields its fruit in its season, and its leaf does not wither. In all that he does, he prospers."

What part of this week's verse stood out to you the most?

_____

_____

MAIN INSIGHT OR TAKEAWAY

What truth or lesson did God highlight for you through the devotional?

_____

_____

_____

PERSONAL APPLICATION

How will you apply this to your business or leadership this week?

_____

_____

_____

CHALLENGES OR CONVICTIONS

Did anything convict, challenge, or stretch you?

_____

_____

_____

ANSWERED PRAYERS / PRAISE REPORT

Did you see God show up in any way this week?

_____

_____

_____

PRAYER FOR THE WEEK

Write a personal prayer based on your reflection.

_____

_____

_____

NEXT STEP OR ACTION ITEM

What's one specific action you'll take based on this reflection?

_____

_____

_____

VERSE

PROVERBS 13:22– *"A good person leaves an inheritance for their children's children."*

INTERPRETATION:

Godly legacy goes beyond financial inheritance—it includes values, vision, and the spiritual foundation we lay for future generations.

DEVOTIONAL THOUGHT

Income is important, but legacy is eternal. As Christian entrepreneurs, we have a chance to leave behind more than money—we can pass down faith, integrity, and purpose through how we build and lead.

APPLICATION

Ask yourself this week, "What am I building that will outlast me?" Start documenting values, principles, and systems that reflect your Kingdom-minded leadership.

REFLECTION

What do you want people—especially your family and team—to remember most about your leadership?

PRAYER

Father,

Direct me to build a business that serves people and honors You for generations to come. May my life and work plant seeds of righteousness and legacy.

Amen.

WEEK 41

SCRIPTURE FOCUS
PROVERBS 13:22– "A good person leaves an inheritance for their children's children."
What part of this week's verse stood out to you the most?

_____

_____

_____

MAIN INSIGHT OR TAKEAWAY
What truth or lesson did God highlight for you through the devotional?

_____

_____

_____

PERSONAL APPLICATION
How will you apply this to your business or leadership this week?

_____

_____

_____

CHALLENGES OR CONVICTIONS
Did anything convict, challenge, or stretch you?

_____

_____

_____

ANSWERED PRAYERS / PRAISE REPORT
Did you see God show up in any way this week?

_____

_____

_____

PRAYER FOR THE WEEK
Write a personal prayer based on your reflection.

_____

_____

_____

NEXT STEP OR ACTION ITEM
What's one specific action you'll take based on this reflection?

_____

_____

_____

VERSE

PROVERBS 10:9 – *"Whoever walks in integrity walks securely, but whoever takes crooked paths will be found out."*

INTERPRETATION

Compromise may bring temporary gain, but it erodes trust and long-term stability. Integrity protects and sustains your business.

DEVOTIONAL THOUGHT

In moments of pressure—financial strain, competition, temptation—it's easy to justify small compromises. But one compromise leads to another. God calls us to walk securely in integrity, even when it costs us.

APPLICATION

Review a recent decision or policy. Was it fully in line with your values? If not, make a correction today.

REFLECTION

Where are you tempted to compromise—and how can you strengthen your stand for integrity?

PRAYER

Lord,
Keep my heart aligned with Yours. Give me courage to do what's right, even when it's hard. I purpose that my business is built on trust, honesty, and unwavering values.
Amen.

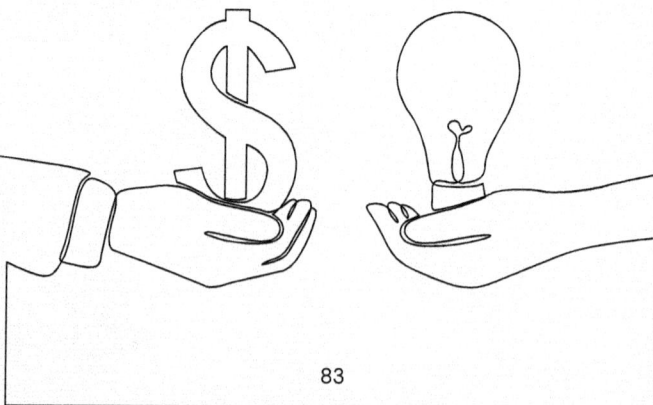

SCRIPTURE FOCUS

PROVERBS 10:9 – "Whoever walks in integrity walks securely, but whoever takes crooked paths will be found out."
What part of this week's verse stood out to you the most?

MAIN INSIGHT OR TAKEAWAY

What truth or lesson did God highlight for you through the devotional?

PERSONAL APPLICATION

How will you apply this to your business or leadership this week?

CHALLENGES OR CONVICTIONS

Did anything convict, challenge, or stretch you?

ANSWERED PRAYERS / PRAISE REPORT

Did you see God show up in any way this week?

PRAYER FOR THE WEEK

Write a personal prayer based on your reflection.

NEXT STEP OR ACTION ITEM

What's one specific action you'll take based on this reflection?

VERSE

EXODUS 18:21 – *"But select capable men from all the people—men who fear God, trustworthy men who hate dishonest gain—and appoint them as officials..."*

INTERPRETATION

Even Moses needed help. God's plan for leadership includes delegation to faithful, capable people who carry the mission forward.

DEVOTIONAL THOUGHT

Entrepreneurs often feel the weight of doing everything. But healthy leadership means trusting others with responsibility. Delegation isn't weakness—it's wisdom. Surround yourself with people who share your values and vision.

APPLICATION

Identify one task or area this week that you can delegate to a trusted person. Let go with confidence and focus on what only you can do.

REFLECTION

What keeps you from delegating—and what could become possible if you did?

PRAYER

Father,
Teach me to lead like You—by equipping and empowering others. I trust the team You've provided and release control in faith.
Amen.

SCRIPTURE FOCUS

EXODUS 18:21 – "But select capable men from all the people—men who fear God, trustworthy men who hate dishonest gain—and appoint them as officials..."

What part of this week's verse stood out to you the most?

_____

_____

MAIN INSIGHT OR TAKEAWAY

What truth or lesson did God highlight for you through the devotional?

_____

_____

_____

PERSONAL APPLICATION

How will you apply this to your business or leadership this week?

_____

_____

_____

CHALLENGES OR CONVICTIONS

Did anything convict, challenge, or stretch you?

_____

_____

_____

ANSWERED PRAYERS / PRAISE REPORT

Did you see God show up in any way this week?

_____

_____

_____

PRAYER FOR THE WEEK

Write a personal prayer based on your reflection.

_____

_____

_____

NEXT STEP OR ACTION ITEM

What's one specific action you'll take based on this reflection?

_____

_____

_____

VERSE

1 THESSALONIANS 5:18 – *"Give thanks in all circumstances; for this is God's will for you in Christ Jesus."*

INTERPRETATION

Gratitude is a posture, not a reaction. It honors God regardless of circumstances and keeps our hearts anchored as we grow.

DEVOTIONAL THOUGHT

Success can tempt us to pride or self-reliance. But gratitude brings us back to humility. It reminds us who brought the increase. Whether you're seeing fruit or still planting seeds, gratitude fuels joy.

APPLICATION

Start or revisit a gratitude journal this week. Write down three things you're thankful for in your business each day.

REFLECTION

How has God been faithful in your journey—and how can you thank Him today?

PRAYER

God,

Thank You for every blessing, big or small. Keep my heart grateful in every season. Keep my business reflecting my trust and thankfulness in You.

Amen.

WEEK 44

SCRIPTURE FOCUS
1 THESSALONIANS 5:18 – "Give thanks in all circumstances; for this is God's will for you in Christ Jesus."
What part of this week's verse stood out to you the most?

MAIN INSIGHT OR TAKEAWAY
What truth or lesson did God highlight for you through the devotional?

PERSONAL APPLICATION
How will you apply this to your business or leadership this week?

CHALLENGES OR CONVICTIONS
Did anything convict, challenge, or stretch you?

ANSWERED PRAYERS / PRAISE REPORT
Did you see God show up in any way this week?

PRAYER FOR THE WEEK
Write a personal prayer based on your reflection.

NEXT STEP OR ACTION ITEM
What's one specific action you'll take based on this reflection?

VERSE

ROMANS 12:2 (ESV) – *"Do not be conformed to this world, but be transformed by the renewal of your mind, that by testing you may discern what is the will of God, what is good and acceptable and perfect."*

INTERPRETATION

Paul calls believers to reject worldly thinking and allow God's truth to shape their thoughts, decisions, and direction. Transformation begins in the mind—when we surrender our assumptions, fears, and ambitions to the renewing power of God's Word, our lives (and businesses) begin to reflect His will.

DEVOTIONAL THOUGHT

Your mindset drives your methods. A renewed mind produces a refreshed mission—and leads to a business that glorifies God.

APPLICATION

Begin each day in Scripture to renew your thinking before the world speaks into it. Challenge thoughts rooted in fear, scarcity, or pride—and replace them with truth. Make space for godly voices and mentors who sharpen your mindset and purpose. Evaluate business goals and methods: Are they conformed to culture or transformed by faith?

REFLECTION

Are your thoughts leading your business toward God's will—or the world's agenda? Where have you conformed to unhealthy patterns of striving, fear, or control? What daily habit could you implement to renew your mind intentionally?

PRAYER

Father,

I give You my mind, my thoughts, and my plans. Transform the way I think so I can lead in a way that pleases You. Help me recognize lies and replace them with truth. May every decision in my business come from a place of clarity, peace, and alignment with Your will. Amen.

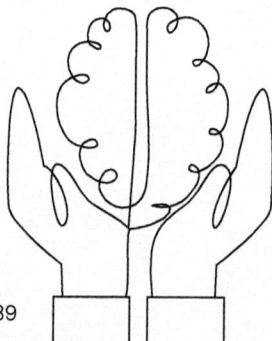

SCRIPTURE FOCUS

ROMANS 12:2 (ESV) – "Do not be conformed to this world, but be transformed by the renewal of your mind, that by testing you may discern what is the will of God, what is good and acceptable and perfect."

What part of this week's verse stood out to you the most?

_____

_____

MAIN INSIGHT OR TAKEAWAY

What truth or lesson did God highlight for you through the devotional?

_____

_____

_____

PERSONAL APPLICATION

How will you apply this to your business or leadership this week?

_____

_____

_____

CHALLENGES OR CONVICTIONS

Did anything convict, challenge, or stretch you?

_____

_____

_____

ANSWERED PRAYERS / PRAISE REPORT

Did you see God show up in any way this week?

_____

_____

_____

PRAYER FOR THE WEEK

Write a personal prayer based on your reflection.

_____

_____

_____

NEXT STEP OR ACTION ITEM

What's one specific action you'll take based on this reflection?

_____

_____

_____

VERSE

DEUTERONOMY 8:18 — *"But remember the Lord your God, for it is He who gives you the ability to produce wealth."*

INTERPRETATION

God is the source of your ability, creativity, and wealth. And with that provision comes the responsibility to steward it for His Kingdom.

DEVOTIONAL THOUGHT

Profit is NOT a dirty word—it's a tool. When earned with integrity and used with generosity, it becomes a powerful resource for impact. Let your profits serve people and purpose, not just personal gain. This may mean taking a great vacation to pour into our family as well as doing good in our communities and for others.

APPLICATION

This week, examine your giving. Could you increase generosity through your business— whether financially or with time, influence, or service?

REFLECTION

How can your business profits be aligned with eternal purposes? Do you have a plan? If not, now is the time!

PRAYER

God,

Thank You for the ability to create value and earn income. I will use all You've given to bless others, advance Your Kingdom, and steward profit with purpose.

Amen.

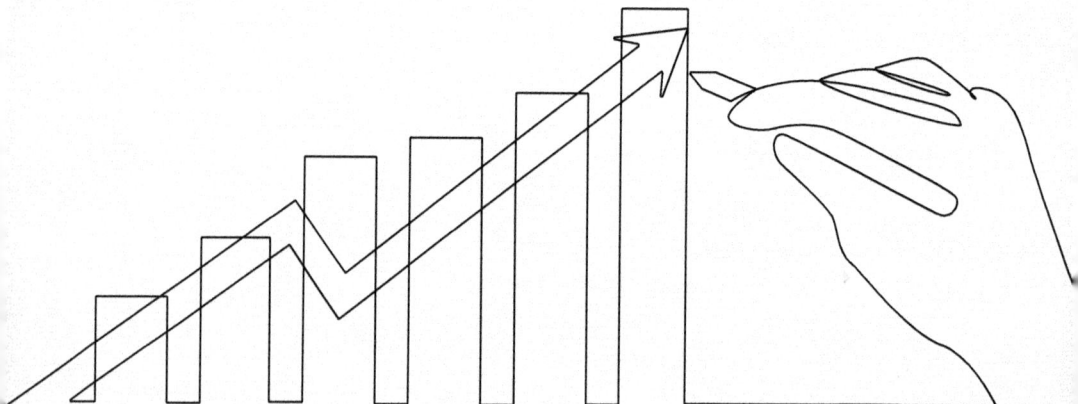

WEEK 46

SCRIPTURE FOCUS
DEUTERONOMY 8:18 – "But remember the Lord your God, for it is He who gives you the ability to produce wealth."
What part of this week's verse stood out to you the most?

_____
_____
_____

MAIN INSIGHT OR TAKEAWAY
What truth or lesson did God highlight for you through the devotional?

_____
_____
_____

PERSONAL APPLICATION
How will you apply this to your business or leadership this week?

_____
_____
_____

CHALLENGES OR CONVICTIONS
Did anything convict, challenge, or stretch you?

_____
_____
_____

ANSWERED PRAYERS / PRAISE REPORT
Did you see God show up in any way this week?

_____
_____
_____

PRAYER FOR THE WEEK
Write a personal prayer based on your reflection.

_____
_____
_____

NEXT STEP OR ACTION ITEM
What's one specific action you'll take based on this reflection?

_____
_____
_____

VERSE

ISAIAH 41:10 – *"So do not fear, for I am with you; do not be dismayed, for I am your God. I will strengthen you and help you."*

INTERPRETATION

God promises presence and strength even in moments of rejection or loss. What feels like an end may be His redirection.

DEVOTIONAL THOUGHT

Rejection hurts—whether from a client, a pitch, or an opportunity lost. But it's not the end. Sometimes God closes doors to protect or redirect you. Don't internalize rejection—anchor your worth in Christ.

APPLICATION

Revisit a recent rejection. Instead of seeing it as failure, ask God to reveal what He's doing through it.

REFLECTION

What rejection are you still holding onto—and how might God be using it for your good? What door was opened as this one was closed?

PRAYER

Father,
Heal the places in me that hurt from rejection. Remind me of who I am in You, and for I commit to move forward with grace and faith. Help me to see, with clarity, the path you want me to follow.
Amen.

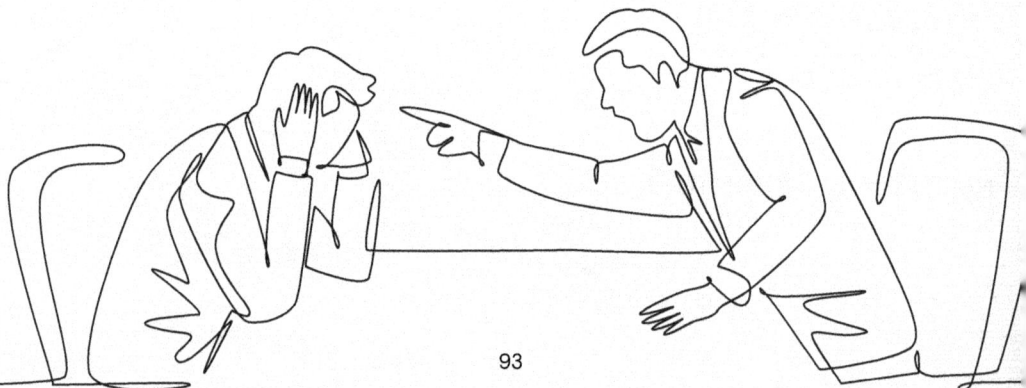

SCRIPTURE FOCUS

ISAIAH 41:10 – "So do not fear, for I am with you; do not be dismayed, for I am your God. I will strengthen you and help you."

What part of this week's verse stood out to you the most?

_____

_____

MAIN INSIGHT OR TAKEAWAY

What truth or lesson did God highlight for you through the devotional?

_____

_____

_____

PERSONAL APPLICATION

How will you apply this to your business or leadership this week?

_____

_____

_____

CHALLENGES OR CONVICTIONS

Did anything convict, challenge, or stretch you?

_____

_____

_____

ANSWERED PRAYERS / PRAISE REPORT

Did you see God show up in any way this week?

_____

_____

_____

PRAYER FOR THE WEEK

Write a personal prayer based on your reflection.

_____

_____

_____

NEXT STEP OR ACTION ITEM

What's one specific action you'll take based on this reflection?

_____

_____

_____

VERSE

PROVERBS 29:18 (KJV) – *"Where there is no vision, the people perish..."*

INTERPRETATION

Vision gives direction, purpose, and endurance. Without it, we drift. With it, we move forward with clarity and conviction.

DEVOTIONAL THOUGHT

Your business needs more than goals—it needs God-given vision. When He breathes life into your future plans, they gain eternal weight. Let your vision be shaped by faith, not just ambition.

APPLICATION

Take time this week to pray over the next year. Write or revisit a vision statement for your business rooted in Kingdom impact.

REFLECTION

Is your current vision God-breathed—or just goal-driven? Work to find the balance.

PRAYER

God,

Renew my vision. Help me see beyond today and dream with You. Direct my business to reflect Your purpose in the world.

Amen.

SCRIPTURE FOCUS

PROVERBS 29:18 (KJV) – "Where there is no vision, the people perish..."
What part of this week's verse stood out to you the most?

MAIN INSIGHT OR TAKEAWAY

What truth or lesson did God highlight for you through the devotional?

PERSONAL APPLICATION

How will you apply this to your business or leadership this week?

CHALLENGES OR CONVICTIONS

Did anything convict, challenge, or stretch you?

ANSWERED PRAYERS / PRAISE REPORT

Did you see God show up in any way this week?

PRAYER FOR THE WEEK

Write a personal prayer based on your reflection.

NEXT STEP OR ACTION ITEM

What's one specific action you'll take based on this reflection?

VERSE

2 CORINTHIANS 9:7 – *"Each of you should give what you have decided in your heart to give, not reluctantly or under compulsion, for God loves a cheerful giver."*

INTERPRETATION

Giving is an act of worship. God delights in generosity that flows from joy, not guilt or pressure.

DEVOTIONAL THOUGHT

Generosity changes atmospheres. As a Christian business owner, you have the privilege to shape a culture of giving—through tithes, bonuses, support, or simply showing up for someone in need.

APPLICATION

Look for one opportunity this week to be generous, in a word, time, or money. Make it intentional and do it joyfully.

REFLECTION

What does joyful giving look like in your business this week? Who or what will you pour into?

PRAYER

Lord,

Make me a cheerful giver. Let my business overflow with generosity that reflects Your love and abundance.

Amen.

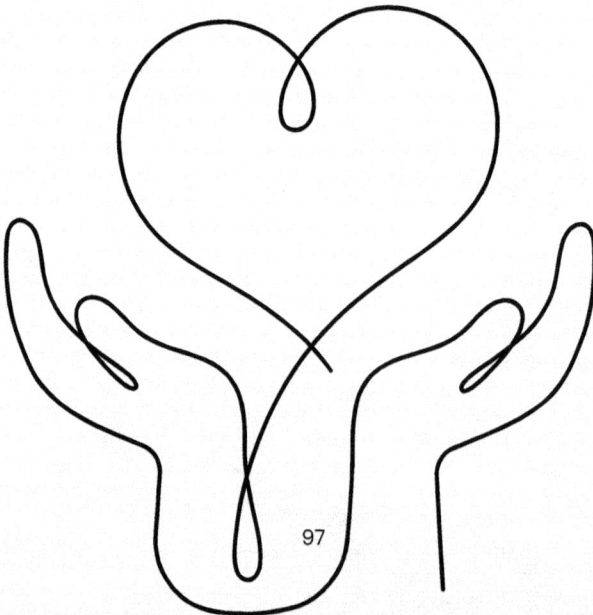

SCRIPTURE FOCUS

2 CORINTHIANS 9:7 – "Each of you should give what you have decided in your heart to give, not reluctantly or under compulsion, for God loves a cheerful giver."

What part of this week's verse stood out to you the most?

_____

_____

MAIN INSIGHT OR TAKEAWAY

What truth or lesson did God highlight for you through the devotional?

_____

_____

_____

PERSONAL APPLICATION

How will you apply this to your business or leadership this week?

_____

_____

_____

CHALLENGES OR CONVICTIONS

Did anything convict, challenge, or stretch you?

_____

_____

_____

ANSWERED PRAYERS / PRAISE REPORT

Did you see God show up in any way this week?

_____

_____

_____

PRAYER FOR THE WEEK

Write a personal prayer based on your reflection.

_____

_____

_____

NEXT STEP OR ACTION ITEM

What's one specific action you'll take based on this reflection?

_____

_____

_____

VERSE

JOEL 2:25 – *"I will repay you for the years the locusts have eaten..."*

INTERPRETATION

God is a restorer. Seasons of loss, delay, or failure are not the final word. In His time, He can redeem and restore what seemed wasted.

DEVOTIONAL THOUGHT

Every entrepreneur has faced loss—of income, opportunity, or momentum. But God specializes in restoration. He brings beauty from ashes and purpose from pain. Trust Him to restore more than what was taken.

APPLICATION

Reflect on a loss you've experienced in business. Surrender it to God again and ask Him for fresh vision and healing.

REFLECTION

Where do you need restoration in your business or spirit today?

PRAYER

Lord,
I give You every loss, failure, and disappointment. Thank You that You restore and repay what the enemy tried to steal. Breathe new life into what's been broken.
Amen.

SCRIPTURE FOCUS
JOEL 2:25 – "I will repay you for the years the locusts have eaten…"
What part of this week's verse stood out to you the most?

_____

_____

_____

MAIN INSIGHT OR TAKEAWAY
What truth or lesson did God highlight for you through the devotional?

_____

_____

_____

PERSONAL APPLICATION
How will you apply this to your business or leadership this week?

_____

_____

_____

CHALLENGES OR CONVICTIONS
Did anything convict, challenge, or stretch you?

_____

_____

_____

ANSWERED PRAYERS / PRAISE REPORT
Did you see God show up in any way this week?

_____

_____

_____

PRAYER FOR THE WEEK
Write a personal prayer based on your reflection.

_____

_____

_____

NEXT STEP OR ACTION ITEM
What's one specific action you'll take based on this reflection?

_____

_____

_____

VERSE

REVELATION 12:11 – *"They triumphed over him by the blood of the Lamb and by the word of their testimony..."*

INTERPRETATION

Your story has power. It is a weapon against darkness and a light to others. When shared with humility and faith, it reveals God's goodness.

DEVOTIONAL THOUGHT

As a business leader, your testimony can inspire employees, partners, and peers. Don't hide the challenges God has carried you through. Speak of His faithfulness. Someone needs the hope you've lived.

APPLICATION

Write or share a part of your testimony this week—how God showed up in your business journey. Be on the look-out for someone who needs to hear this to help them on their journey.

REFLECTION

What part of your story would encourage someone else if you shared it?

PRAYER

Father,

Thank You for the story You are writing in my life. I commit to speak of Your goodness with boldness and grace. Use my testimony to bring hope to others.

Amen.

WEEK 51

SCRIPTURE FOCUS
REVELATION 12:11 – "They triumphed over him by the blood of the Lamb and by the word of their testimony…"
What part of this week's verse stood out to you the most?

MAIN INSIGHT OR TAKEAWAY
What truth or lesson did God highlight for you through the devotional?

PERSONAL APPLICATION
How will you apply this to your business or leadership this week?

CHALLENGES OR CONVICTIONS
Did anything convict, challenge, or stretch you?

ANSWERED PRAYERS / PRAISE REPORT
Did you see God show up in any way this week?

PRAYER FOR THE WEEK
Write a personal prayer based on your reflection.

NEXT STEP OR ACTION ITEM
What's one specific action you'll take based on this reflection?

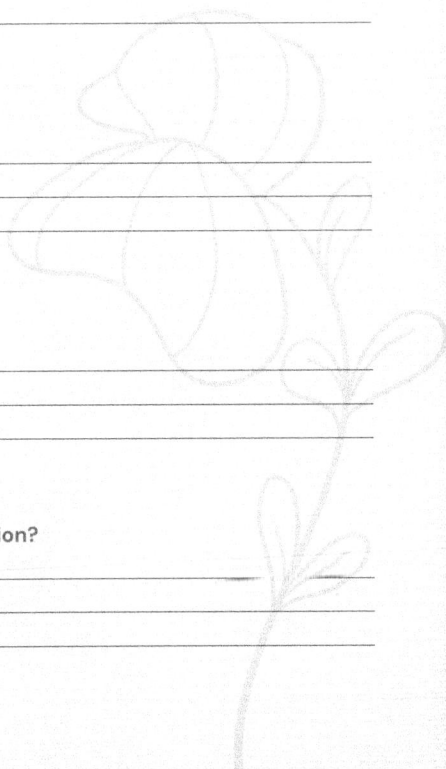

VERSE

PHILIPPIANS 1:6 – *"He who began a good work in you will carry it on to completion until the day of Christ Jesus."*

INTERPRETATION

God finishes what He starts. As one chapter ends, He's already preparing the next. You're not alone in finishing well or starting again.

DEVOTIONAL THOUGHT

Ending a season—whether a year, a project, or a pivot—can feel uncertain. But God's work in you isn't done. Celebrate the victories, grieve the losses, and step into the new with faith. He is faithful to complete it.

APPLICATION

Take time to journal the key lessons, blessings, and breakthroughs from this year. Then ask God what He wants to begin in the next and pay attention!

REFLECTION

What has God completed this year and what might He be beginning in you? Have you set your new year's resolution? Do you have a plan?

PRAYER

Lord,
Thank You for walking with me every step of
this journey. I trust You with the finish and the
fresh start. Complete Your good work in me and
through my business.
Amen.

WEEK 52

SCRIPTURE FOCUS
PHILIPPIANS 1:6 – "He who began a good work in you will carry it on to completion until the day of Christ Jesus."
What part of this week's verse stood out to you the most?

MAIN INSIGHT OR TAKEAWAY
What truth or lesson did God highlight for you through the devotional?

PERSONAL APPLICATION
How will you apply this to your business or leadership this week?

CHALLENGES OR CONVICTIONS
Did anything convict, challenge, or stretch you?

ANSWERED PRAYERS / PRAISE REPORT
Did you see God show up in any way this week?

PRAYER FOR THE WEEK
Write a personal prayer based on your reflection.

NEXT STEP OR ACTION ITEM
What's one specific action you'll take based on this reflection?

DEAR READER,

As you close out this 52-week journey, I want to offer my deepest gratitude for inviting this devotional into your life and business. It has been an honor to walk with you—week by week, scripture by scripture—as you align your work with your faith.

Whether you've read these devotionals over coffee before the start of your day or reflected on them in moments of rest or uncertainty, I pray they've helped remind you that you are never alone in business. God is in your strategy, your setbacks, your success, and your surrender. He is the true CEO, the ultimate Provider, and the greatest source of wisdom.

Thank you for saying "yes" to building something that not only serves others but glorifies Him. Thank you for leading with integrity, choosing obedience over comfort, and walking the hard road of entrepreneurship with Kingdom purpose. Your faithfulness matters more than you know.

If this devotional has encouraged you, I'd love to hear your story. Keep leading with courage and conviction. Keep showing up, sowing faithfully, and trusting God for the harvest.

With gratitude and prayer,

David Mosberg

Entrepreneur & Author